JONATHAN EDWARDS

The Great Awakener

Helen K. Hosier

BARBOUR
PUBLISHING, INC.
Uhrichsville, Ohio

Other books in the "Heroes of the Faith" series:

Gladys Aylward	*Martin Luther*
William and Catherine Booth	*D. L. Moody*
John Bunyan	*Samuel Morris*
William Carey	*George Müller*
Amy Carmichael	*Watchman Nee*
George Washington Carver	*John Newton*
Fanny Crosby	*Mary Slessor*
Jim Elliot	*Charles Spurgeon*
Charles Finney	*Corrie ten Boom*
Billy Graham	*Mother Teresa*
C. S. Lewis	*Sojourner Truth*
David Livingstone	*John Wesley*

©MCMXCIX by Barbour Publishing, Inc.

ISBN 1-57748-559-9

Scripture quotations are taken from the Authorized King James Version of the Bible.

Published by Barbour Publishing, Inc., P.O. Box 719, Uhrichsville, OH 44683 http://www.barbourbooks.com

Member of the
Evangelical Christian
Publishers Association

Published in the United States of America.

JONATHAN EDWARDS

introduction

The great nineteenth-century historian George Bancroft claimed that anyone wishing to know the workings of the eighteenth-century New England mind "must give his days and nights to the study of Jonathan Edwards." Revivalist, theologian, philosopher, man of letters, pastor, missionary, college president, and beloved husband and father, Jonathan Edwards was destined to become the controversial figure of his generation.

Today, however, that reputation has somewhat dimmed. According to Ralph G. Turnbull, "Moderns know little about him except that he is spoken of as a preacher of 'hell-fire.'" (Turnbull's reference is to one of Edwards's sermons, and probably *the* most famous so-called hell-fire sermon ever preached, entitled "Sinners in the Hands of an Angry God.") But Jonathan Edwards was so much more than that sermon, and his reputation as a preacher whose messages were largely mingled with terror and vengeance is unwarranted and unjust. "It is not by the fig-ure of the sinner dangling over the pit of hell by which we should recall his realistic preaching," Turnbull continues, "but the sinner *in the hands of God*, the hands which also offered mercy and grace, hands which were wounded and nail-pierced at the Cross of Calvary." To judge him in any other way is not to do justice to the man.

One cannot claim ignorance of Edwards based on a lack of dependable source material. On the contrary, his life is among the best documented of all Americans of the eighteenth century. For a start, there are over 1,100 of his sermons existing in their original manuscript form. There are the many books, some partly historical, pub-lished by Edwards in his lifetime. There is some autobi-ographical material, a portion of a diary, and about 200 of his letters. Beyond all this, there is the testimony of many eyewitnesses and other contemporaries and the many biographies published since his death in 1758.

Perhaps the lukewarm reception can be traced to Jonathan Edwards's outspoken Puritan and Calvinist the-ology. Following in the great tradition of Puritan piety, Jonathan proclaimed fearlessly the distinction between God and man, or rather, that man is ungodly. Certainly the radical distinction between the human and the divine is the centerpiece of his theology. But if one delves deeper, there is another layer waiting to be discovered, and Edwards wrote—and preached—extensively concerning the hope of man. For while man is not God and cannot make himself godly, he can be made godly. Man deserves punishment, yet on occasion God has determined to redeem him or those predestined to receive salvation.

Unlike his Puritan predecessors, Edwards was able to combine scientific and philosophic concepts—particularly those of Isaac Newton and John Locke—to explain theological dogma. From Newtonian principles, Edwards could more clearly explain the magnificence of God; from Lockean thought, he was able to articulate how man experienced God directly but passively. And from these deductions, Edwards was able to establish the pillars of his Christian faith: man's inherent depravity, God's absolute sovereignty, the predestination of all souls, and the free and unearnable gift of God's saving grace to those whom He has forechosen.

As Iain H. Murray explains, "The division [concerning Edwards] runs right back to the Bible, and, depending on where we stand in relation to Christ, we shall join ourselves to one side or the other in interpreting this man who was, first of all, a Christian."

The truth is, Jonathan Edwards divided men in his lifetime, and he continues to divide his biographers to this day. "The nature of his greatness, the significance of his life and thought, an assessment of his character and writings—on all these, and much else, judgments are divided," Murray writes.

How shall we think of Jonathan Edwards? Certainly, for starters, as the premier Christian thinker of the North American continent. The historian Peter Gay, who saw Edwards as the most wasted, obsolete, and irrelevant mind of his century, has lamented about "all that brain power going to waste in the mind of a man who liked to think about God!" He has been likened to the great nineteenth-century Danish philosopher and psychologist of religion

Soren Kierkegaard. Both were towering figures, yes, giants, in the art and science of examining sin, guilt, anxiety, and the abyss. Edwards, however, is recognized as expounding the sweetness of grace and the goodness of salvation. He was, in the words of Harold P. Simonson, a great man "because of the intrinsic value of his own mind, the integrity of his thinking."

The quality of Jonathan Edwards's life was intense and dramatic. As his enormous legacy of writings almost defies description, so his "resume" seems equally mind-boggling. He was a preacher bearing the responsibility of perhaps the most influential congregation in the thirteen colonies, at Northampton, Massachusetts Bay Colony; he was a missionary to the Housatonic Indians and pastor in Stockbridge of the same colony; he was a major part of swelling revivals, including the Great Awakening of 1740–1742; he was (for five weeks) college president in Princeton, New Jersey; and, moreover, he was husband to the gracious Sarah Pierrepont and father to eight daughters and three sons. All of this, and so much more, in the brief life span of fifty-five years (1703–1758).

As a young man, Jonathan Edwards wrote a series of seventy resolutions, and one of them is especially telling. *"Resolved,"* he wrote, "To live with all my might, while I do live." Jonathan Edwards believed that man's life is of eternal consequence. Indeed, Murray found Edwards's life and writings to be very relevant to this present period in the history of the church. According to Murray, Edwards believed, for example, "that the age of scientific discovery was only in its beginnings and that there would come new and better contrivances for assisting one another through the whole earth by more expedite, easy, and safe communication between distant regions than now." Murray says Edwards would not have been surprised had he known of the great advances of the kingdom of Christ in the two centuries that have followed his death.

A word or two on style is in order. When quoting from works from the eighteenth century, I have often retained the quaint manner of spelling, capitalization, and punctuation (or lack of it), which represents the Puritan style. Where confusion might result, the correct spelling and punctuation have been substituted.

Because most materials on Jonathan Edwards are in the public domain, I have chosen to omit the use of footnotes. Where authors or sources are mentioned, please consult the bibliography at the end of the book for pertinent publishing information. The absence of dialogue between the characters is by no means accidental. The Puritan dialect of Edwards's era does not lend itself easily to constructing conversations for today's reader. In fact, there is very little conversational tone in work done by others on him.

It has been my prayer throughout the writing of this book that God would be pleased to allow me to portray this giant of the faith in a readable fashion. However, because Edwards was given to wordiness, I have sought, therefore, to extract what I considered to be the most thought-provoking material, shortening sentences by the use of ellipses (. . .), without compromising what Edwards was conveying.

My hope is that you will gain a sense of the greatness of this man whose writings and spirit centuries cannot dim, a man who found "sweet delight in God and divine things."

—Helen K. Hosier

one

"Father, I've finished my composition," said the twelve-year-old lad as he handed his writing to his father, the Reverend Timothy Edwards, who was also the schoolmaster in East Windsor, Connecticut Colony.

The school was, in fact, in the family's parsonage "parlour." In a room equipped on three sides with benches fastened to the wall, Jonathan Edwards and his sisters, together with village boys, including his Stoughton family cousins, received their elementary education.

At this moment Jonathan's cousins were particularly attentive. The sons of Captain Thomas Stoughton, who was married to Timothy's sister Abigail, the seven boys—three of whom were older, three younger, and one almost the exact age of Jonathan himself—lived in the house nearest the Edwardses. They had most definitely played a role in what preceded the writing of Jonathan's essay. *What would Reverend Edwards think of Jonathan's choice of subject matter?* Jonathan had explained to them that spiders were the "corrupting nauseousness of the air," a phrase he borrowed from eavesdropping on his elders. But he had also held their rapt attention for hours on end, sharing his clear-sighted observations as to the spider's ballooning habits, and his inspired guess as to the liquid character of the unspun web.

"Thank you, Jonathan," his schoolmaster-father said, taking the sheaf of papers from the boy. Glancing at them, his interest was immediately observed by eight pairs of eyes. "Hmm. . .well. . . ," he uttered, and then read the title aloud, "Of Insects." Jonathan shifted his standing position. He'd worked many long hours on this particular essay and he hoped for his father's favorable comments.

"You've been observing the spiders, I see," his father continued. "This is very well done, my son, I think I'm going to learn a lot about these insects."

"Yes, Father, I've been watching them from the prayer booth and out in the woods and the fields." The village was surrounded by densely wooded forests, spacious meadows, and a brook. The Edwardses' home stood on land that sloped gently down to this brook. Somewhere along this brook Jonathan and his cousins had built a booth in which they would meditate and pray. Like a modern-day treehouse, the booth was also their secret site to watch the activities of spiders. Thus, writing of spiders was quite natural for a boy who had a long and deep intimacy with nature.

Although Jonathan returned to his bench and lessons, the schoolmaster's eyes were intently focused on the words before him: "Multitudes of times I have beheld with wonderment and pleasure the spiders marching in the air from one tree to another," Jonathan had written, "their little shining webbs and Glistening Strings of a Great Length and at such a height as that one would think they were tack'd to the Sky by one end were it not that they were moving and floating. . . ."

It wasn't the first occasion the Reverend Timothy Edwards had found himself astounded by the philosophic speculations of his only son. There had been the time, for instance, when Jonathan had handed him the essay entitled "Of the Rainbow." Timothy was amazed how the boy's mind was filled with the wonder of the world around him. Jonathan could see at an early age that God revealed Himself in the beauty of the Connecticut hills as truly as in a sanctified heart. The strength of rocks, the movement of clouds, the color of rainbows, the sweet taste of honey, the fascination with spider webs—these things didn't escape young Jonathan's attention.

(Succeeding generations have shown that Jonathan Edwards displayed in "Of Insects" a truly remarkable scientific sense. Indeed, his observations of flying spiders were so accurate that they have been preserved and acknowledged in the scientific community. It should be remembered that his findings were those of a boy who had no training in scientific observation, no microscope, and no body of specialized knowledge by which to test his observations and conclusions.)

Jonathan's manner of determining answers even as a young boy shows his mental development, as several biographers have noted. In his words, he "became very conversant with Spiders" by spending long hours in the woods—exploring rotten logs, tracking down and classifying the various kinds of spiders he found, and always seeking to understand how these insects stretched their webs from tree to tree. He was never able to rest until he finished what he had begun. Then and only then did he draw final conclusions, discussing his theory with his sisters and cousins and enlisting their help in watching spiders as well so as to corroborate his observations.

He came to the conclusion that if all the insects hatched their young in the infinite plenitude with which they lay their eggs, the whole visible world would in time become choked with insects; no other form of life could possibly exist. There must be, therefore, some law or principle of nature that maintains the insect population in proper balance with the rest of creation. He watched butterflies on the wing and the spiders carried aloft on their filmy threads and saw that the prevailing westerly winds carried hordes of these insects out to the Atlantic Ocean where, presumably, they were drowned. "The chief end of this faculty, that is given them," he wrote, "is not their recreation, but their destruction." He reasoned that the movements of these insects are caused not only by air currents and seasonal changes, but by an "intervention" which he explained as the laws of nature operating in the eternal intention God had for the universe from the beginning of time. Years later he preached on the spider as one of the four things on earth that are exceeding small and yet exceeding wise.

Thinking back upon his childhood, Jonathan wrote years later, "I had a variety of concerns and exercises about my soul from my childhood. When I was yet a child, no children's play to me was pleasing; all my mind was set serious to learn and know. . . ." Instead his mind was occupied with thoughts of God and concern for things that were divine and eternal. As Turnbull has stated, "We shall never know all the workings of that strange and lightening mind, but we can believe that in youth there walked in New England an unusual life with the qualities of spiritual genius upon his brow."

This genius was more than demonstrated in another essay written by young Jonathan entitled "Of Being." He reasoned correctly that human consciousness suffers from gaps in its thinking. It cannot think all the time — it sleeps, it dreams, it has blanks. Yet, thought is continuous: From hour to hour and day to day the business of thinking proceeds even if the subject of cognition (the act or process of knowing including both awareness and judgment) is for a time abandoned. So what fills these skipped intermediaries in thought? Jonathan asked and pursued the idea until the answer came, an answer rich in spiritual insight and natural observation. The God who animates all of nature holds thought in reserve until man's mind is ready or nature's activity is favorable in order that the right thought or act will be released in man or the realm of nature at just the right time.

Certainly God had blessed Jonathan with a keen mind, but the influence of Timothy Edwards was also a divine gift. Typical of most New England ministers of his era, Reverend Edwards considered his "school" one of his regular duties. He was a diligent and patient tutor, albeit strict and demanding, who wanted his students and his own children, in particular, "to excel in the things of the Lord." The methods by which the children were taught were common to the times in which they lived. Children started memorizing Latin at age seven. The importance of writing was also ingrained in the students, and this habit was to remain with Jonathan throughout his life.

When Jonathan was approaching eight years of age, Timothy Edwards was conscripted to serve as chaplain in the "Queen Anne's War," and the duties of teaching the children, in addition to all her other responsibilities, fell to Mrs. Edwards. A letter dated August 7, 1711, from Timothy contains guidance for his wife on many matters —the old rope for the well needed to be replaced, one of the horses required special care, the cattle must be kept out of the orchard, and manure needed laying before winter. But the children were uppermost in his mind: "I desire thee to take care that Jonathan don't lose what he hath learned but that as he hath got the Accidence, and above two sides of *propria quae moribus* [Latin exercises] by heart so that he keep what he hath got, I would therefore have him say [recite] pretty often to the girls. . . ."

Latin was not Timothy Edwards's chief concern for Jonathan: "If any of the children should at any time go over the river to meeting I would have them be exceeding careful how they sit or stand in the boat lest they should fall into the river. . . . I hope thou wilt take special care of Jonathan that he don't learn to be rude and naughty, etc., of which thee and I have lately discoursed."

It has been said that Jonathan's East Windsor boyhood was "fair seed-time" for the soul of a philosopher. His nurturing father and mother, his large extended family, and the expanse of nature that greeted him each day were all part of those early years. And then there was his innate frontier spirit, passed down from his forebears who had bravely stretched the boundaries of their world for a better life.

two

Jonathan Edwards's known heritage extends back through four generations with his earliest roots in England. While biographers for years have eagerly and persistently sought to link him with similarly distinguished names, their efforts have been, for the most part, without success. Edwards's family background may be considered typical of well-educated New England clergymen of the eighteenth century.

His great-great-grandfather, Richard Edwards, was a respected university man and an ordained minister with both Bachelor's and Master's degrees from St. John's College, Oxford. As rector in the small parish church of Ratcliffe, a position that carried with it the dignity and social prestige of a Church of England living, Richard was a well-regarded man of the cloth. Before his untimely death from the plague in 1625, he and his wife, Anne, had one son, William.

Three months later, his widow married James Cole, cooper. A cooper by definition is someone who makes or repairs wooden casks or tubs—a good business in those days. James cultivated a fine relationship with his step-son, as evidenced by an incident that happened in 1634, nine years after his marriage to Anne Edwards. Having met with serious financial reverses, James was forced to flee London to escape punishment. In a letter to his wife he wrote, "I do desire to have the biggest child with me," and that meant sixteen-year-old William.

William was offered a shilling by a kindly neighbor and joined his stepfather in his self-imposed exile. Together the two shared hardships and fear of prison, but they were together, and that was all that mattered. James Cole valued Christian liberty and worship in a church where, as he wrote, "there is neither Crosses nor Surplus, nor kneeling at the Sacrament nor the booke of common prayer nor any of these behaviours but reading the word Singing of psalms prayr before and after Sermon with Catichisme." What James had expressed was commonly called Dissenting Doctrine, a belief characterized by ardent followers who militantly opposed ritualistic worship. Such was the influence upon William Edwards, great-grandfather of Jonathan Edwards, during his most impressionable years.

Cole's longing for peace and liberty was undoubtedly the motivating force that propelled him, his wife, Anne, William Edwards, and his own children, James, Abigail, and Timothy, to migrate to the shores of America. They arrived during the latter part of 1635, and records show they were in the party of Thomas Hooker that traveled to the Connecticut Valley. When they reached the Connecticut River—"the long river," as the Indians had aptly named it—they settled at a site that they named Hartford, fifty miles inland from the mouth of the river. There James prospered sufficiently with his cooper's trade, saving enough to pay off his English debts. In time, he purchased land, built his family a fine home, and taught his stepson William Edwards the cooper's trade. Upon his death in 1652, he left his wife a legacy of three annual pounds, which proved sufficient for her needs as she survived him by twenty-seven years.

William Edwards, the first generation of the Edwards line in New England, was a man of modest attainments, but nonetheless a workman whose cooper's mark was a guarantee of skill and integrity. He married Agnes Spencer, a widow, sometime between 1642 and 1645. Little is known about their married life in the house beside the cooper's shop. They had one son in 1647 whom they named Richard for his paternal grandfather.

Richard Edwards lived in Hartford for all his seventy-one years, long enough to see the town change from a frontier settlement to a prosperous commercial center, and long enough also to see his soon-to-be famous grandson enter college. Indeed, that was perhaps a high point in his rather sad and tragic life.

Richard's wife, Elizabeth Tuttle, to whom he was married for twenty-four years and who bore him six children, was "not of sound mind." They were married in 1667, and three months later she named under oath before two magistrates the father of her unborn child. Richard bore his travail decently and quietly, but after repeated infidelities, on October 9, 1690, he filed a petition for divorce on scriptural grounds and was refused. However, after careful review, the divorce was granted on October 8, 1691, a deeply significant case and one almost without parallel in seventeenth-century America. A gentleman of remarkable restraint, Richard Edwards was generations ahead of his time when, in setting down the cause for his legal action, he was unwilling to detail in writing the specifications of his wife's "folly."

As a businessman, Richard accumulated extensive holdings in land, cattle, oxen, horses, and farm equipment. His considerable wealth was reflected in his elegant Hartford home, one "appropriate" for his station in life. His son Timothy, Jonathan's father, described Richard as "a stalwart man of noble stature and comely countenance, erect, robust and nimble to an unusual degree, good in argument, pleasant in consultation and well furnished for society."

His second marriage at age forty-five to Mary Talcott, daughter of Lieutenant John Talcott, one of the original settlers of Hartford, was very different from his first. Before his death in 1718, he and Mary enjoyed twenty-seven years together, and always Richard was noted for his silence and unassailable dignity.

Timothy, the son of Richard and Elizabeth, was sent to live in the home of the Reverend Pelatiah Glover of nearby Springfield before he enrolled at Harvard College. Actually, the reverend received students in divinity, but it might be that young Timothy's father sought and found a way to remove his son from the home environment, which may have been anything but pleasant.

College records show that Timothy Edwards received two degrees—Bachelor's and Master's—on July 4, 1694, and that he graduated with distinction. Two months later, he married Esther Stoddard and began what at first was to be a trial period at the second church in the far-flung settlement of Windsor. The position, however, lasted sixty-four years, from 1694 until his death in 1758.

At the beginning of the eighteenth century, East Windsor was still considered part of the frontier, due to the real, if lessening, threat of Indian attacks. As Ola Winslow observes, "Not for another generation could a child grow up without the memory of a thousand cautions as to what was by no means a phantom danger." The town limits were considered the "very boundaries of life," and for good reason. When Jonathan Edwards was only four months old, his mother's half-sister, Eunice Williams, and two of her children were murdered in the infamous Indian raid at Deerfield, Massachusetts, and her husband and four children were taken captive. Not long before Timothy arrived in the village, churchgoing men were still required to bring their muskets inside the meetinghouse, just in case they might be needed.

Despite a rather undistinguished pastorate, and one at times characterized by dissension, Timothy showed remarkable judgment in his choice of a spouse. Esther Stoddard was the second child of the much-esteemed Reverend Solomon Stoddard and of Esther Warham Mather, daughter of John Warham, first minister to Connecticut Colony, and widow of the Reverend Eleazar Mather. The Stoddards were a long-lived clan, and Jonathan's mother was to prove no exception. She came

21

as a bride to East Windsor at age twenty-three and lived to be ninety-eight years old in this same village. While she was recognized as having unusual intellectual abilities, her husband's many tributes of affection indicate that she possessed sweetness as well as strength.

Four daughters had already been born into the family home when Jonathan, Timothy and Esther's first and only son, came along on October 5, 1703. Six more daughters would follow him. Considering his family heritage and the fact that he was the only son, there was no doubt that Jonathan—a name that means "gift of Jehovah"—would become a clergyman. For as surely as he signaled the continuation of the Edwards name, he also represented a new link in a family of honest free-thinkers and dedicated spiritual leaders. But in those austere pulpits of England and New England where his predecessors had rigidly stood, Jonathan Edwards would distinguish himself. Under the cloak of Puritanism, he would start a fire—and a passion—to truly know God.

three

The Reformation that swept through Europe changed the face of Christianity forever and laid the foundations of the later great expansion into the New World. The names of Luther, Zwingli, and Calvin became known far and wide, with Calvinistic doctrines exerting the most influence on the Puritan mind.

The Puritan philosophy, which became known as Covenant Theology, was ingrained in Jonathan Edwards almost from birth. The Covenant Theology was based on several unassailable tenets. First, the all-powerful and all-wise Creator gave all creatures the same purpose: to serve and glorify God. While human beings occupied the highest station in creation, they were still servants of God and were committed to what was called the Covenant of Works.

However, due to Adam's sin in the Garden of Eden, when he chose to serve himself and his own selfish desires instead of God, the Covenant of Works was broken. Yet God is merciful as well as just, and this is demonstrated by His attitude toward Abraham. God told Abraham that his seed would prosper, and that has been realized by God's gift of a Redeemer who would atone for Adam's sin. This Redeemer would restore order in creation, provide a path from misery to happiness, and repair the relationship between man and God. This Redeemer is, of course, Jesus Christ.

The promise of God's Redeemer created a new covenant between God and man, called the Covenant of Grace. God no longer required works for salvation; He simply asked for belief, or faith, in the Redeemer. At the same time, God provided man with the means to believe, through the gift of the Holy Spirit. The Holy Spirit would grant individuals grace, or the power to have faith. But saving faith, in the Calvinist-Puritan view, was not open to all. In His wisdom, God elected certain men and women to obtain salvation.

As the eighteenth century progressed, there was a listlessness toward a strong commitment to these tenets. Certainly, the Reverend Timothy Edwards and his astute wife sensed the stirrings of a new religious climate.

From 1620, when the first Pilgrim fathers began to settle on the coastline of Massachusetts, until the early 1700s, the colonists were united in their desire to escape the intolerant society of England. There was a distinct feeling that these brave settlers were the chosen people and that although far from the country of their birth, still they were close to God. And they had prospered.

But early in the eighteenth century there appeared in

the New England colonies to be an indifference to the Christian faith. Alister E. McGrath speaks of New England Puritanism as having lost its way. The future of Christianity in the New World seemed to be in doubt. Older Christians had become intensely nostalgic, longing for the old days of their youth when there was such a passionate concern for spiritual renewal and growth.

Early rumblings of this indifference fell upon the ears of young Jonathan. As loyal descendants of the Puritans increasingly insisted upon the need for a reawakening of that early religious life, awareness sprung up inside him of the importance of such a mission.

But it was difficult for Jonathan to find time to think about such things in the busy—and crowded—life of the parsonage home. All of Jonathan's ten sisters grew to six feet in height, causing the townspeople to refer to them as Timothy Edwards's "sixty feet of daughters." And if eleven children weren't enough, there were frequent visitors who made the Edwards home a regular stopping point on their journeys.

Ever cautious, Jonathan still managed to find solace in the meadows and woods near his home. In giving an account of his conversion, experiences, and religious exercises, he spoke of this period in his life:

I had a variety of concerns and exercises about my soul from my childhood; but had two remarkable seasons of awakening, before I met with that change, by which I was brought to those new dispositions, and that new sense of things, that I have since had. The first time was

25

when I was a boy, some years before I went to
college, at a time of remarkable awakening in
my father's congregation. I was then very much
affected for many months, and concerned about
the things of religion, and my soul's salvation;
and was abundant in duties. I used to pray five
times a day in secret, and to spend much time in
religious talk with other boys; and used to meet
with them to pray together. I experienced I know
not what kind of delight in religion. My mind
was much engaged in it, and had much self-
righteous pleasure; and it was my delight to
abound in religious duties.

This was the time when he and his friends built a
booth in a swamp, in a very secret place, which they used
for a place of prayer. Jonathan explains, "My affections
seemed to be lively and easily moved, and I seemed to be
in my element, when engaged in religious duties."

To Jonathan, religion must be more than "religion,"
but an individual experience of the heart responding to
the promptings of the Holy Spirit, and in his case urging
him toward solitary times of deep introspection. Going
to the meetinghouse and keeping the Sabbath as the son
of the pastor was expected to keep it—these were not
enough.

As he spent more time in thought, a stumbling block
arose in his mind about certain doctrines, and he spoke
freely of this with his father. He told him of the objections he harbored against the doctrine of God's sovereignty, in choosing whom He would to eternal life, and

rejecting whom He pleased, "leaving them eternally to perish, and be everlastingly tormented in hell." However, after much introspection Jonathan goes on to write:

> . . .But only. . . now I saw further, and my reason apprehended the justice and reasonableness of it. However, my mind rested in it; and it put an end to all those cavils and objections, that had 'til then abode with me, all the preceding part of my life. And there has been a wonderful alteration in my mind, with respect to the doctrine of God's sovereignty, from that day to this; so that I scarce ever have found so much as the rising of an objection against God's sovereignty, in the most absolute sense, in showing mercy to whom He will show mercy, and hardening and eternally damning whom He will. God's absolute sovereignty, and justice, with respect to salvation and damnation, is what my mind seems to rest assured of, as much as of any thing that I see with my eyes.

The working-out of that doctrine was a major turning point in his life, or as he called it, a "first conviction." He goes on to explain another sense he experienced that he called "a delightful conviction." He referred to this as an "inward, sweet delight in God and divine things, that I have lived much in since," and it happened while he was reading these words from 1 Timothy 1:17: "Now unto the King eternal, immortal, invisible, the only wise God, be honour and glory for ever and ever. Amen."

*As I read the words, there came into my
soul, and was as it were diffused thro' it, a sense
of the glory of the Divine Being; a new sense,
quite different from any thing I ever experienced
before. Never any words of scripture seemed to
me as these words did. I thought with myself,
how excellent a being that was; and how happy
I should be, if I might enjoy that God, and be
wrapt up to God in Heaven, and be as it were
swallowed up in Him. I kept saying, and as it
were singing over these words of scripture to
myself; and went to prayer, to pray to God that I
might enjoy Him; and prayed in a manner quite
different from what I used to do; with a new sort
of affection.*

Jonathan was left with a new idea of Christ, the work
of redemption, and the glorious way of salvation by Him.

*My mind was greatly engaged, to spend my
time in reading and meditating on Christ; and the
beauty and excellency of His person, and the
lovely way of salvation, by free grace in Him. . . .
I found, from time to time, an inward sweetness,
that used, as it were, to carry me away in my
contemplations; in what I know not how to
express otherwise, than by a calm, sweet abstrac-
tion of soul from all the concerns of this world;
and a kind of vision, or fix'd ideas and imagina-
tions, of being alone in the mountains, or some
solitary wilderness, far from all mankind, sweetly*

28

*conversing with Christ, and wrapt and swallowed
up in God. The sense I had of divine things,
would often of a sudden as it were, kindle up a
sweet burning in my heart; an ardor of my soul,
that I know not how to express.*

Such was the depth of his adolescent spiritual experience, an experience that would color all his thoughts
and writings in later years and set him apart from his
contemporaries. Indeed, Turnbull believes the spiritual
disciplines and soul struggle that took place at this juncture in Jonathan Edwards's life are comparable to those
experienced by Augustine and Pascal.

When he was almost thirteen years old, having com-
pleted his studies at home, childhood officially ended for
Jonathan. He had recited his last lesson in the "parlour"
and was now ready for college.

But those thirteen years had determined many things.
He had a very sober view of life with a distinct reflective
bent. He was extremely self-disciplined and things per-
taining to God and His plan of salvation, the Bible, and
matters of a religious nature were the unquestioned
goals of his life. His mind was already his servant; he
knew how to think for himself. He would not easily be
swayed by the opinions of others. His calling was a
straight path before him.

He was to leave his beloved father—his mentor,
teacher, and spiritual guide—for the esteemed professors of the Collegiate School (two years later to be
known as Yale College). But Timothy Edwards would
never be far from his thoughts.

The disciplines of language and literature given by his father equipped him for college. Jonathan's father had in fact prepared several boys for higher learning and established a reputation as such a proficient teacher that college admission tutors remarked that "there was no need of examining Mr. Edwards's scholars."

Jonathan was to exchange his one-room schoolroom in his parental home for a much more pretentious place. However, the great, yawning chasm separating life as it had been from life as it was to be would not deter the young scholar. His roots had gone down deep not only in New England soil, but into the love of God.

Impressed upon his mind were the great religious arguments of his youth. Impressed upon his heart, however, was a searing passion for a true relationship with Jesus Christ and a need for revival.

four

The years 1716 to 1720 were a time of discovery for Jonathan. There was an intensity about his life, as reflected in his writings, that reveals agony as well as jubilation in God's felt presence, but there was also some dread and even terror leading to bouts of melancholy, rebellion, and despair. Perhaps contributing to his inner turmoil was his current milieu. Yale College was still in the throes of being born. Founded in 1701, the Collegiate School, or Yale College, was only two years older than Jonathan himself.

Up until Jonathan's arrival, the school had been located in Saybrook, Connecticut. The question of its removal to New Haven was the subject of heated debate at just the time Jonathan entered the freshman class. In fact, shortly after Jonathan's arrival in New Haven, the class was moved to Wethersfield for two years, and then back to New Haven for his junior and senior years. Plots and counterplots were swirling about the new higher institution as rival villages entertained hopes of becoming the permanent seat of the college.

Through those years Jonathan established himself as a well-disciplined student, but a loner for the most part, who kept himself absorbed in his reading and studies—in truth, he walked to the tune of a different drummer.

Perhaps the peak of his experience at Yale was his discovery of John Locke's *Essay on the Human Understanding*. At last Jonathan had found a kindred spirit. Locke confronted him with ideas, with *philosophy*. A new world was opened and his copybook came alive. Pen in hand, Jonathan became critic as well as pupil.

This intellectual awakening of his mind, the reasoning, the questioning, and his step-by-step thought process set down in unpunctuated sequence, are found in two early compositions, one entitled *The Mind* and the other, *Notes on Natural Science*. These essays, written by Jonathan as a sixteen-year-old senior, were excursions into the realm of thought that was to be his greatest work for the rest of his life. "One thing that may be a good help towards thinking profitably is, when I light on a profitable thought, that I can fix my mind on, to follow it as far as possibly I can to advantage."

At an earlier age he had experienced difficulties with the problem of language when seeking to speak of "things of Christianity," things "so spiritual, so refined." How could he bridge the natural and the spiritual? Later, he was to say that it was because of this breakdown of language that he attributed "most of the jangles about religion in the world." Simply stated, he was always to struggle with this intense desire to express the sense of his heart through words in order to excite this sense of the heart in others. But now, with youthful determination, he pounced on Lockean theories, declaring them to be valuable, even like "handfuls of silver and gold."

Jonathan Edwards was impressed with Locke's analysis of language—of words, of ideas—and the deterioration of language that takes place when words lose their anchorage in ideas. Both Jonathan and John Locke recognized that as a consequence, people often mouth empty words. But Locke failed to provide answers to the deeper thinking of young Jonathan's heart. There was an unremitting drive in him for spiritual truth rather than mere aesthetic elegance. Later, as a preacher, he was to declare his own method was a plain style consisting of faith-language and that God "has been pleased to smile upon and bless a very plain unfashionable way of preaching and that it ever has been, and ever will be, God's manner, to bless the foolishness of preaching to save them that believe. . . ." This helps to explain why his preaching found such favor once he launched upon his life work as a pastor.

Locke's primary influence on Jonathan was not as a model but as a goad. Sensible knowledge for Edwards meant heart-knowledge. Simonson explains that Edwards was convinced that the basis of language must be existential, that is, a tying of words to experience and a sending of living stuff into them. "Like fruit to the vine," Simonson said, "words have their life only in their final oneness with the heart."

Jonathan Edwards would have liked that statement—

and he would have added that it was all of grace. That it was the Spirit of God at work in a man's heart, that mere theological terms such as salvation, faith, sin, judgment, covenant, or any other rhetorical embellishments a preacher might add and use, will never take the listener to the final truth (locked within these words) unless divine grace has first empowered his heart to sense that which the language signifies. Then and then only did Edwards consider such language and the redeemed heart as one.

During his final days at Yale, confusion swirled around him. Discussions regarding orthodoxy, church polity, and other troublesome issues were being raised, yet Jonathan seemed to know his goals in life and stayed focused. He graduated in September 1720 at the head of a class of ten with a Bachelor of Arts degree. He then stayed an additional two years, taking theological studies to prepare him for a license to preach. In September 1723 he was granted the degree of Master of Arts from Yale College. He was eighteen years old and open to a church appointment.

Yale had done much to activate his mind. Now he was exhilarated not only by the little and wondrous things of nature but by what was more important, the activity of a mind capable of knowing and discovering a world quite on its own. To Jonathan, the senses are merely the windows of the mind; they are given to man fresh and even free each time a human being is born. A man at any age should be able to come alive each morning, to stand on tiptoe against the sun's rising or the rain's falling, and to close each day as if nothing like it

34

had ever existed before or would ever come again. One could thank God for the nearly intoxicating revel of the senses, for God had given them to man and they were nearly divine.

The future stretched before him. Where would he go? How would he conduct himself in the "real world" of men and ideas? Locke's writings had been, as it were, a wake-up call, an appeal to the uniqueness of the mind that would become Jonathan Edwards's theme for a lifetime.

Life, as he saw it, whatever its length, would not be long enough for the grace of God to work its way with him and for him to share this with others.

five

Two years as a graduate student of theology at Yale had prepared Jonathan for the ministry but not for life in the metropolis of New York. Since 1626, when the early Dutch immigrants had purchased Manhattan Island from the Indians—just one hundred years earlier—New York was well on its way to becoming the bridge between Europe and the American West, a virtual clearing-house between the Old World and the wilderness of the New World.

One would think that this place of ships, exotic languages and dialects, different dress and mannerisms, and crowded streets would have captured the mind of eighteen-year-old Jonathan Edwards. Yet from the records of his life, there is no evidence to suggest that he was very interested, at least at the outset. The secular had never been of any consequence to him. Obviously God had His hand on this young man, his heart and his thinking, and he was not distracted by what was going on in the world.

Jonathan had been called to serve a group of parishioners who had seceded from the First Presbyterian Church on Wall Street near Broadway. This small Scotch Presbyterian parish became, under his ministrations, something very akin to the village pastorate in East Windsor. It would appear that the Connecticut Colony had been very friendly with the struggling Scotch Presbyterians and that the call to him might naturally have come to a candidate from Yale College. Lacking a zest for exploration and no curiosity about New York's people and their doings, Jonathan gave himself wholly to this new position, to what he called his "eager pursuit after more holiness and sweet conformity to Christ."

During this time he wrote what he called his *Personal Narrative*, or a diary of his spiritual pursuit, and his thoughts literally spilled out onto its pages.

> *I had vehement longings of soul after God*
> *and Christ, and after more holiness; wherewith*
> *my heart seemed to be full, and ready to break:*
> *which often brought to my mind, the words of the*
> *Psalmist, Psalm 119:20, "My soul breaketh for*
> *the longing that it hath. . ."*
>
> *My mind was greatly fix'd on divine things; I*
> *was almost perpetually in the contemplation of*
> *them. Spent more of my time in thinking of*
> *divine things. Prayer seem'd to be natural to*
> *me; as the breath, by which the inward burnings*
> *of my heart had vent.*

In speaking of his preaching in New York, he explained that "very sensibly, in a much higher degree [than he had experienced before]" his longings after God and holiness "were much increased."

Pure and humble, holy and heavenly
Christianity, appeared exceeding amiable to me.
I felt in me a burning desire to be in every thing
a complete Christian; and conformed to the
blessed image of Christ: and that I might live in
all things, according to the pure, sweet and
blessed rules of the gospel.

He asked himself how he could be more holy, how he could live "with vastly more earnestness." So great was this pursuit that it began to manifest itself in physical discomforts that were eventually to prove "a great damage to me," as he wrote. He planned his life very carefully in order to secure spiritual fervor, eating and drinking moderately and asking himself every night whether he had succeeded. In his efforts to transform himself from a mere man to a vehicle for the Spirit of God, he sometimes showed a lack of discernment in matters relating to health and bodily needs.

Reality, however, pressed upon him in the friendship of John Smith, who was a member of his congregation, and his mother. John apparently was a simple person, "A Currier in Queen Street" (as records show), employed about the docks near where the little church was located. In fact, for a time Jonathan lived with John and his mother. Very little is known about any such friendships that Jonathan cultivated, so this relationship is noteworthy. How much John Smith contributed to Jonathan Edwards's thinking, enabling him to understand and better address his sermons to these common folk, is not known; what is known is that John's friendship provided a joyful experience for him, as evidenced by his writing.

> *I had then abundance of sweet religious conversation in the family where I lived, with Mr. John Smith, and his pious mother. My heart was knit in affection to those, in whom were appearances of true piety; and I could bear the thoughts of no other companions, but such as were holy, and the disciples of the blessed Jesus.*

Perhaps as a result of the Smiths, Jonathan began to take more of an interest in the goings-on in the world around him. "I had great longings for the advancement of Christ's kingdom in the world," he wrote. "My secret prayer used to be in great part taken up in praying for it. If I heard the least hint of any thing that happened in any part of the world, that appear'd to me, in some respect or other, to have a favorable aspect on the interest of Christ's kingdom, my soul eagerly catch'd at it; and it would much animate and refresh me. I used to be earnest to read public news-letters, mainly for that end; to see if I could not find some news favorable to the interest of religion in the world."

He referred to the delight he still had in "retiring to a solitary place, on the banks of the Hudson River, at some distance from the city, for contemplation on divine things, and secret converse with God" and how he had "many sweet hours there." Sometimes he and John Smith would walk there together, through the streets of the old Dutch town, with cobblestones so sharp that pedestrians had to tread carefully, and out into the meadows by the Hudson, conversing about "the things of God; and our conversation used much to turn on the advancement of Christ's kingdom in the world, and the glorious things that God would accomplish for his church in the latter days."

Jonathan's time in New York eventually became one of spiritual refreshment as the Bible became "the greatest delight. . .of any book whatsoever." Every word seemed to touch his heart. "I felt an harmony between something in my heart, and those sweet and powerful words. I seem'd often to see so much light, exhibited by every sentence, and such a refreshing ravishing food communicated, that I could not get along in reading. Used oftentimes to dwell long on one sentence, to see the wonders contained in it; and yet almost every sentence seemed to be full of wonders."

When Jonathan made the decision to leave this New York church after seven short months, he wrote: "My Heart seemed to sink within me at leaving the Family and City where I had enjoyed so many sweet and pleasant Days." The reasons for his departure are unclear. While the New York church was believed to have difficulties meeting its financial obligations, a letter months later written to Jonathan by a church administrator confirms the parish's regret at his leaving but also their anticipation of a new, and perhaps better qualified, preacher.

Undoubtedly the motivating force behind the young man's departure was the Reverend Timothy Edwards. Wanting his son to be in the best possible position to be the likely heir to the esteemed Solomon Stoddard (then in his eighties), Timothy had paved the way for a preaching position for Jonathan in Bolton, Connecticut, not far from East Windsor. Stoddard was widely regarded as the leading spiritual authority in the Connecticut Valley, so much so, in fact, that people were prone to call him "Pope Stoddard" behind his back. Was Timothy forseeing the day when Grandfather Stoddard's weighty mantle would rest on young Jonathan's shoulders?

Since December, Jonathan had carried on a grudging correspondence with Bolton, even though he was in no hurry to leave New York. Why he left when he did is perhaps the greater mystery: Jonathan would not sign an agreement with the Bolton church until November 1723. Jonathan's diary records his departure in the following way: "I went from New York to Wethersfield by water. As I sail'd away, I kept sight of the city as long as I could; and when I was out of sight of it, it would affect me much to look that way, with a kind of melancholy mixed with sweetness. However, that night after this sorrowful parting, I was greatly comforted in God at Westchester, where we went ashore to lodge: and had a pleasant time of it all the voyage to Saybrook. It was sweet to me to think of meeting dear Christians in heaven, where we should never part more. At Saybrook we went ashore to lodge on Saturday, and there kept sabbath; where I had a sweet and refreshing season, walking alone in the fields."

The transition back into New England life found him with his thoughts clarified on many points, as evidenced by his "Resolutions," which he had started writing during his undergraduate years at Yale and continued during his seven-month sojourn in New York. This collection of exhortations to himself contains two telling entries, numbers forty-three and forty-four, which reveal a profound dedication of himself to God for life:

43. *Resolved, Never, hence-forward, till I die, to act as if I were any way my own, but entirely and altogether God's agreeable to what is to be found in Saturday, Jan. 12th, 1723.*
44. *Resolved, That no other end but religion, shall have any influence at all on any of my actions; and that no action shall be, in the least circumstance, any otherwise than the religious end will carry it. Jan. 12, 1723.*

To what "religious end" God was leading him he had no idea. Like many young men and women of today who return home to live after college, Jonathan's primary concern was adjusting to life with his parents—after his first tantalizing taste of independence.

six

His mother and father, his sisters still remaining at home, his cousins and friends, and his father's parish—all this awaited and welcomed Jonathan Edwards back to East Windsor in May of 1723. He'd been gone all told seven years, including his time in college.

After he had been at home a few days, he found it necessary to subdue "a disposition to chide and fret," acknowledging in his diary that he was still too quick "to manifest my own dislike and scorn." The very next entry reveals that he resolved "never to allow the least measure of any fretting or uneasiness at my father and mother" to affect any facet of his behavior. Weeks later, Jonathan penned that he had decided to replace his "air of dislike, anger and fretfulness" with an "appearance of love, cheerfulness, and benignity." Further, he wrote that he had "sinned in not being careful enough to please my parents."

Translated, that may have meant accepting cheerfully the pastoral position in Bolton, the one his father had desired for him. Thus, on November 11, 1723, Jonathan signed a settlement agreement in the Bolton town record book. Clearly, the arrangements to keep him as their permanent pastor had been made and everything was in readiness: Salary, wood, pastureland, and a homestead had been provided.

But a short time later, Jonathan inexplicably left Bolton for East Windsor. After more months of living and waiting at home, he accepted a position as a tutor at Yale College and arrived in New Haven in May 1724. The position, while not that of a pastor, had ministerial overtones. Jonathan would be responsible for the discipline as well as instruction of the notoriously undisciplined undergraduates.

There may also have been another consideration for Jonathan's acceptance of the Yale appointment—and her name was Sarah Pierrepont of New Haven. Sarah was the daughter of James Pierrepont, first minister in New Haven and one of the original movers in the founding of Yale College. Her mother, who also came from a notable ministerial line, was the granddaughter of Thomas Hooker, considered "an eminent divine" and leader of the 1630 migration to the Connecticut Valley. Hooker had founded the town of Hartford, and it is believed he brought with him (as noted earlier) William Edwards, cooper, first of the Edwards line in America.

While little is to be found about her in the writings of and about Jonathan Edwards, he did know her already when she was thirteen and, in fact, wrote a striking bit of poetic prose about her when he was twenty. Fortunately, that tribute has been preserved. She must have cherished it, referring to it often while Jonathan was in New York.

They say there is a young lady in [New Haven] *who is beloved of that Great Being, who made and rules the world, and that there are certain seasons in which this Great Being, in some way or other invisible, comes to her and fills her mind with exceeding sweet delight, and that she hardly cares for anything, except to meditate on Him—that she expects after a while to be received up where He is, to be raised up out of the world and caught up into heaven; being assured that He loves her too well to let her remain at a distance from Him always. There she is to dwell with Him, and to be ravished with His love and delight forever. Therefore, if you present all the world before her, with the richest of its treasures, she disregards it and cares not for it, and is unmindful of any pain or affliction. She has a strange sweetness in her mind, and singular purity in her affections; is most just and conscientious in all her conduct; and you could not persuade her to do anything wrong or sinful, if you would give her all the world, lest she should offend this Great Being. She is of a wonderful sweetness, calmness and universal benevolence of mind; especially after this Great God has manifested Himself to her mind. She will sometimes go*

about from place to place, singing sweetly; and
seems to be always full of joy and pleasure; and
no one knows for what. She loves to be alone,
walking in the fields and groves, and seems
to have some one invisible always conversing
with her.

Sarah Pierrepont was certainly well worthy of Jonathan's affections and regard. In his *Life and Character of the Late Reverend Mr. Jonathan Edwards* (Boston, 1765), a sketch by Samuel Hopkins states, "Hers was a nature not only of remarkable susceptibility to religious impression, but of executive force, cheerful courage, social grace, and sweet, womanly leadership." Other biographers relate that she was noted for her charm, flashing wit, and light sparring with words. Still, she regarded piety as the goal of life and pursued the "things of religion" with a single-mindedness that always set her apart from those of her own age.

Although Jonathan was to hold the position of tutor for two years, it was a time of great mental and spiritual stress despite his productive work for the college. Feeling himself responsible to right the wrongs of the college problems he had inherited from previous individuals, he put himself under sterner rigors of self-discipline, even denying himself food and sleep. It was inevitable that after little more than a year (sixteen months to be exact) he became severely ill and nearly lost his life.

Explaining this difficult time in his life, Jonathan Edwards reflected that he had "sunk in his religion; my mind being diverted from my eager and violent pursuits after holiness, by some affairs that greatly perplexed and distracted my mind."

Thus it was in September 1725 that he endeavored to go home to East Windsor but was taken so ill at the North Village that he could go no farther. "I lay sick for about a quarter of a year. And in this sickness, God was pleased to visit me again with the sweet influences of His Spirit. My mind was greatly engaged there on divine, pleasant contemplations, and longings of soul."

Thoughts of heaven and words from the Gospels, particularly the holiness of God, God's mercy, the Holy Spirit, the way of salvation by Christ, and the absolute sovereignty of God consumed Jonathan Edwards. They were restorative in their power, and three months later he returned to his work at Yale.

Once again he encountered the troubles that still rocked the college, dating as far back as the 1722 insur-rection, when leaders of the college had denounced Congregationalism and, in loyalty to the legal govern-ment, declared themselves Episcopalians. Caught in this tangle, he again spoke of "despondencies, fears, per-plexities, multitudes of cares, and distractions of mind." The year 1726 was a very difficult time for the young man. "I have now abundant reason to be convinced of the troublesomeness and vexation of the world, and that it never will be another kind of world," he wrote.

When I find those groanings which cannot be uttered [that] *the Apostle speaks of; and those soul-breakings, for the longing it hath,* [that] *the Psalmist speaks of* [see Psalm 119:20], *to humor*

49

and promote them to the utmost of my power, and
be not weary of earnestly endeavoring to vent
my desires.

To count it all joy when I have occasion of
great self-denial because then I have a glorious
opportunity of giving deadly wounds to the body
of sin, and greatly confirming and establishing
the new nature: to seek to mortify sin, and
increase in holiness, these are the best opportu-
nities, according to January 14.

His reference to January 14 is noteworthy. On that
date he explains:

Great instances of mortification are deep
wounds given to the body of sin, hard blows that
make him stagger and reel; we thereby get great
ground and footing against him.—While we live
without great instances of mortification and self-
denial, the old man keeps whereabouts he was;
for he is sturdy and obstinate, and will not stir
for small blows. After the greatest mortifications,
I always find the greatest comfort.

Facing discouragement as a result of "afflictions of
all kinds," Edwards recognized them as "blessed opportunities of forcibly bearing [me] on in my Christian
course."

He understood the enemy's attacks as meant to
"damp the vigor of my mind, and to make me lifeless,"
but that he could counterattack and seize these times "as

opportunities of trusting and confiding in God, and getting [into] a habit of doing that."

Moreover, he saw the distractions and difficulties as "opportunity of rending my heart off from the world, and setting it upon heaven alone. . .and as a blessed opportunity to exercise patience; to trust in God, and divert my mind from the affliction, by fixing myself in religious exercises."

Also, let me comfort myself, that it is the very nature of afflictions to make the heart better; and if I am made better by them, what need I be concerned, however grievous they seem for the present?

In 1727, as his father fervently hoped, Jonathan was called to share the pulpit with his illustrious grandfather in Northampton, Massachusetts Bay Colony. The decision, largely influenced by Solomon Stoddard himself, had not been a given. Stoddard had many grandsons, and he had not enjoyed a particularly close relationship with Jonathan. It was believed that Jonathan's Yale education, coupled with his albeit brief experience in the pulpit, had turned the tide in his favor.

Shortly thereafter, Sarah Pierrepont accepted an invitation to share her life with a certain up and coming clergyman. Time cannot dim the words of a young man in love awaiting his wedding, no matter how erudite his mind. "Patience," he told his wife-to-be with typical Puritan restraint, "is usually regarded as a virtue, but in this case I think it may almost be considered as a vice."

seven

It was the expectation of many, besides those in his immediate family, that Jonathan Edwards be successor to the Northampton pulpit. Still, the stiff formalities of that era required that he be "called" after he had presented himself as a candidate. After being invited "to assist" the dignified eighty-four-year-old Stoddard, he would then be invited "to settle," and his salary, always subject to increase, and other details would be appropriately taken care of at that time.

Winslow notes that once Jonathan had taken his place among "divines" so seasoned and change-resistant, he was destined almost inevitably to keep within the ministerial pattern as it had been reverenced in America. To the grandsons and great-grandsons of New England's first settlers, the focus was on the present. But to those of Solomon Stoddard's generation, the past was there to cling to, and tradition was first and foremost.

Certainly the ministerial pattern that Jonathan admired had been firmly established by none other than his father, Timothy Edwards. While he never enjoyed the success of his father-in-law, Timothy was nonetheless obsessed with his own pastoral authority, or lack of it. Throughout his years at East Windsor, he was in open conflict with the elders over his own salary and the pastor's right of absolute control within the church. But the issue that would divide pastor and congregation for a large part of his career involved the so-called Saybrook Platform, which Timothy Edwards enthusiastically endorsed. This platform stated that ministers had an absolute veto on church admissions and complete control of the choice of issues to be discussed at church meetings. Undoubtedly Timothy Edwards's obsession with authority had been ingrained in young Jonathan as he proceeded to share the pulpit in Northampton, but would not surface as an issue for years to come.

Jonathan Edwards must have known that someday he would encounter some serious challenges to his pastorate. But Grandfather Stoddard had been a kind of demigod to the Edwards children, and Jonathan made the decision to approach "Stoddard's Way" (of doing things and his doctrinal positions) with a favorable bias. He would be a colleague pastor and accept the existing order, all the while making his own observations.

And what exactly was Stoddard's Way? Solomon Stoddard embraced the Puritan's Covenant Theology, but only in part. Like all good Puritan Calvinists, he believed in the inscrutability and immeasurable glory of God. God had sent His Son to be man's redeemer; by definition, therefore, Christ's righteousness was perfect and sufficient for the salvation of all men, who had only to believe in the truth of Gospel promises. But "all" meant those whom God had predestined for eternal life.

However, Stoddard also believed that God had commanded that He be worshiped by all men, even those not elected for salvation. These men could still use their natural faculties to understand the glory of God and to respond to His majesty. From 1677 Stoddard had interpreted this to mean that no one could be denied access to the church or to the communion table for personal reasons.

Such was Stoddard's influence throughout New England that this "Half-Way Covenant" was soon widely accepted, despite such a free interpretation of Scripture. Then, as now, churches were characterized by conservative and liberal elements, and Solomon Stoddard found himself at the forefront of the more liberal way of thinking. By proposing that the "unregenerate," the non-Covenant members of the community, be allowed to come to and participate in the Lord's Supper along with the converted members, provided only that they were not "scandalous" in their way of life, Stoddard dealt a staggering blow to the defenders of primitive purity in the churches.

Stoddard's vigorous and rational treatises in support of his position were widely read and circulated. Finally, after New England recovered from the first shock, it was seen that Stoddard carried most of New England with him. Soon "Stoddard's Way," as described in his practical argument, "Let the unregenerate come to the Lord's Table; it may help them," was being hailed in parish after parish. The Northampton parish, in particular, continued to flourish and Stoddard's parishioners in general enjoyed the prestige he had brought them.

Records show that Jonathan Edwards was ordained as pastor of the Northampton church on February 15, 1727. There is no account of Jonathan's formal ordination or the reception that followed. No such celebration had occurred for fifty-five years, and it can be presumed that Northampton would have done justice to such an auspicious occasion.

At age twenty-three Jonathan was indeed youthful and inexperienced but at the same time visionary and hopeful. Into this arena he brought his seventeen-year-old bride with almost everything in their favor.

The Pierrepont-Edwards marriage took place in New Haven on July 20, 1727, five months after Jonathan's ordination. In those days it was the custom for a bride to walk to her seat in the meetinghouse in her wedding dress on the first Sunday following her wedding. Certainly the entrance of the beautiful Sarah Pierrepont Edwards would have been an eventful occasion attracting neighboring ministers and parishioners to join in the services and festivities. Indeed, the Northampton parsonage hadn't seen a bride for fifty-seven years!

As noted earlier, Jonathan had grown up with the understanding that the ministry was the highest of all callings and that it conferred honors and prerogatives that were commensurate. It was to be expected, therefore, that the terms of Jonathan's acceptance of the position as Colleague to Solomon Stoddard meant, according to the language of the Town Record, a "Support Suitable & well adapted to that honourable office." Like any other member of "the pulpit fraternity" of his day, Jonathan expected not only a comfortable maintenance and leisure for study, but also the honor and reverence as "befitted a spokesman of God." It followed therefore that he was a man of special privilege.

Three hundred pounds was allotted for settlement initially, and Jonathan used it to buy a homestead on King Street in which he and Sarah and their offspring would live for the next twenty-three years. His salary would be one hundred pounds a year, and more if the value of money declined or if his family increased. There were also ten acres of pastureland "against Slowbridge" and forty acres up the river. A month after his ordination the sum for settlement was increased eighty pounds, and three years later, when Solomon Stoddard died, one hundred pounds was added to the salary.

Needless to say, the Edwards family was well taken care of, but they would need every penny. Jonathan and Sarah were to produce eleven children, eight daughters and three sons, one every two years with Puritanical regularity. It was felt by the Puritans that a happy home was one of the truest proofs of Christianity, and in that respect the Edwards home was exceptionally outstanding. Certainly the greatest fear of both Jonathan and Sarah, as good Puritan parents, was that their children would go to hell. Consequently, from the time she discovered she was with child, Sarah prayed fervently for her baby's salvation.

Jonathan and Sarah's children adored them, and it was noted by many that they rarely had to punish one of their brood. An hour was spent with his family each evening, before the children went to bed and he returned to his study. It was not an hour of devotions so much as a time of good conversation in which everyone participated.

Three of his daughters, Esther, Lucy, and Susannah, were described as possessing "spirited nonsense," a trio who could bring laughter to the household. Yet Jonathan's fatherly instincts found him being quite indulgent with his family—silver spoons for his daughters before they were old enough to use them properly, extra pennies for little Jerusha for her diligence in reading, a gold locket and chain for Mrs. Edwards, playthings for the children.

At the start of their ministry in Northampton, the young couple immediatcly plunged into the work that was set before them in what would have been considered the most prosperous inland community in the Massachusetts Bay Colony. There was much to be done. Solomon Stoddard's energies had been waning, and it was neces-sary for Jonathan to assume more of the responsibility than may have originally been envisioned. Jonathan and Sarah saw disorder among the young people: They recognized the need for children to be catechized and for there to be an emphasis on family religious duties and prayer, and they gave energetic attention to these concerns.

Two years later, on February 11, 1729, the elder Stoddard died. For more than sixty years he had dominated the Connecticut Valley and often contested the ecclesiastical leadership in New England. The mantle, indeed, had now fallen. At his funeral service in Northampton on February 13, most of the ministers within riding distance were in attendance. But although Jonathan was now the heir apparent, he had no role at the service. Instead, the Reverend William Williams of Hatfield, Massachusetts, considered the most eminent of Solomon Stoddard's sons-in-law, delivered the funeral sermon. Little did Williams realize that his words would have a far greater significance in the years to come than perhaps anyone present realized. Sounding a warning to those gathered, Williams advised them "not to idolize men, even the best, the ablest and the wisest" by raising too great expectations from them.

Jonathan was now twenty-five and in charge of the most important parish in western Massachusetts with a congregation numbering over six hundred. He had earned the esteem and respect of the people during his two years as colleague pastor, and to some extent he had their affection. To many of his parishioners, however, he appeared shy and aloof, too absorbed in the things of eternity to indulge in worldly conversation. Yet they liked him—his quiet mannerisms, his eloquence in the pulpit, and his sound doctrine. And when he became seriously ill late in the same year of his grandfather's death, his people showed their concern and built him "a Good Large Barn." Frailty of health and preoccupation with study made it difficult for Jonathan to share much in the labors of his small Northampton acreage, but to a degree he did what he could.

A typical day for the Reverend Jonathan Edwards of Northampton began at four in the morning, when he would rise and light his single candle. For thirteen hours every day he would pore over volumes of theology and perhaps classics of English literature.

After the large midday meal (known as dinner), he might chop wood for exercise, weather permitting, or "set out" trees. On pleasant afternoons he especially liked to get on his horse and ride for three miles to a lovely grove where he would commune with God among the trees. Carrying pen and ink with him, he would dismount and walk, jotting down thoughts that were then reworked at night into what he called the "Miscellanies." On longer horseback rides he would carry with him more papers and pens. After thinking through his ideas and committing them to paper, he would then pin the papers on his coat. Legend has it he would reach home with papers pinned all over his coat and Sarah would have to unpin him!

In the evening he would enjoy an hour's relaxation with Sarah, as the two would sit by the fireside smoking their clay pipes and talking with their children. Breakfast and the evening meal consisted of bread and milk only, with coffee, chocolate, and tobacco as rare luxuries. Meat was eaten once a day, at the midday meal.

Despite his numerous physical afflictions, when he mounted his high pulpit on the Sabbath, Jonathan presented an impressive picture—"tall, spare" with a "deliberate manner [that] gave him a commanding presence." His chief asset was the quality of his voice. According to Hopkins, Edwards's timbre was "very distinct and strangely arresting. He particularly commended the well-placed pauses and great distinctness in pronunciation." John Hooker, a fellow minister, called him "the most eloquent man he ever knew," defining eloquence as "the power of making strong impressions of the subject of a discourse on the minds of an audience." Another, Thomas Prince, spoke of his naturalness of delivery, his low, moderate voice, his freedom from mannerisms, his "habitual and great solemnity, looking and speaking as in the presence of God." Winslow likened his demeanor to that of the philosopher Ralph Waldo Emerson: Both gave the impression of speaking from the immediate inspiration of the moment, in spite of the manuscripts before them.

The making of sermons occupied much of Jonathan's time. His reading, his studies, his thoughts were all centered upon the question, What shall I preach? As he listened to his heart, digesting what he was reading and studying in the Scriptures, he wrote down the answer in his many notebooks. His sermon manuscripts, which came with him into the pulpit, were each carefully written out in a tiny booklet stitched together by hand that was then placed inside the oversized Bible. Made of foolscap (the term used in New England at the time for writing paper), these sermon booklets measured 3 7/8 by 4 1/8 inches. But paper was hard to come by, and it wasn't cheap; it had to be carried on horseback from Boston, and sometimes weeks elapsed before a depleted supply could be replenished.

Making do the best he could, Jonathan's tiny sermon booklets were often written on scraps of paper of all sorts—letter folds, blank sides of letters or documents received, old Yale theses, governors' proclamations, broadsides, bills from Mr. Potwine's general store in Hartford, requests for prayers, and children's copybook exercises—whatever he could find. The busy Reverend

Edwards saved scraps of paper just as he saved scraps of time.

But his schedule was never a deterrent to the many visitors to his home or to the needs of his parish. Indeed, the parsonage often seemed like a wayside inn, with Jonathan and Sarah never turning anyone away. Visitors spoke of his quiet intensity, the gracious hospitality always extended by both the Reverend and Mrs. Edwards, the politeness of the children, and the well-ordered household that Mrs. Edwards oversaw. Sometimes there would be a dozen or eighteen for dinner after a meeting; often the family was awakened at all hours by the sound of horses' hooves and Jonathan would rouse himself and help to take care of the needs of the horses as well as the men. At times the guests would have to remain for a time because of sudden illness or other problems that arose. Joseph Emerson wrote, "Very courteously treated here. The most agreeable Family I was ever acquainted with. Much of the Presence of God here. Mr. Edwards was so kind as to accompany us over Connecticut River and bring us on our way." Such a farewell tradition—to ride out with his guests for a few miles—was Jonathan's special way of extending hospitality.

He did minister faithfully to the needs of his parish and there are many records in his sermon booklets and papers showing requests for prayers, thanksgiving for deliverance, the loss of loved ones, and personal appeals in a variety of distresses, all requests from his parishioners for their pastor's help. He gave little time, however, to visiting the people in their homes. Even so, he kept in touch with his congregation and, when called, would go at once to attend to the needs of the sick and the needy. He was known to hold private meetings in different neighborhoods from time to time, and he always made himself available to the young people in the community for prayer and conversation.

While his early years in Northampton were blessed and prosperous, a spiritual thundercloud was poised above all New England. From his youth Jonathan had been aware of the need for an awakening, but little did he realize the role he had been called to play.

eight

As the Puritan experiment in America neared its centennial anniversary early in the eighteenth century, great changes had taken place in the fabric of life since the founding of the colonies. Nowhere were these changes more evident than in Jonathan Edwards's "backyard" of Northampton.

By the 1730s available land for farming was at a premium. Individual plots of land had already been allocated, and the options available were few. Families could move elsewhere, farther out on the frontier, and then face the very real threat of Indian attacks. Emigration back to England was another none too desirable choice. And then the sons of farmers could patiently wait for their fathers to bequeath them their farms. This final option was compounded by the fact that men (and women) were living longer than ever before. By the time the sons took over the reins of the plows, so to speak, they were often well into middle age.

In this preindustrial society, career choices besides farming were few, and those who did choose a different path had the financial backing of wealthy farming fathers. The difference between the rich and the poor was growing greater year by year, creating mounting frustration, especially among the young people. In short, the traditional rewards the young had dreamed about were no longer there, and they had lost their hope.

Consequently, Edward M. Griffin explains, the zealous commitment of these first generations of New Englanders to the Puritan way of life seemed to have diminished almost to the vanishing point. To counter this trend, many of the loyal descendants of those Puritans, members of the clergy, began to strenuously insist upon the need for a reawakening of that early religious life.

Religion had become sterile, formal, and external. It had been years since Solomon Stoddard had shaken up New England with his radical theological interpretations. A new voice and a new message were needed, and where better to issue the clarion call than from Stoddard's own pulpit!

Now firmly ensconced in the Northampton church, Jonathan Edwards began to issue a nostalgic appeal to days gone by, to a simpler time of life. Decrying the decline of parental authority, Jonathan directed his sermons to the adolescents in his flock, and they began to show, in his words, "a very unusual flexibleness" to his messages.

To bolster his efforts, he advocated singing in worship, an issue that had long divided conservative adults and children throughout New England. Known as "the Singing

Quarrel," the crux of the conflict was whether worshipers could enjoy the "novelty" of singing hymns with tunes from books. Children in Northampton especially enjoyed the Sunday evening services when singing from books was encouraged.

Although at times Jonathan spoke on the great and terrible wrath of God and the urgency of personal salvation, his sermons had more reference to the practical virtues of everyday piety than to anything spectacular. Salvation was a recompense in itself as well as an escape from future torment. "It would be worth the while to be Religious if only for the Pleasantness of it" is a typical sermon theme that can be found in his sermon booklets.

To the surprise of many of the older members of the parish and to Jonathan Edwards's joy, the young people sat up, took notice, listened carefully, and began to mend their ways. Their preacher had something to say and they weren't about to miss it! His words had an irresistible finality. Under the influence of his preaching and example, the youth of the town—many notorious for their religious apathy and their flaunting of the Sabbath by engaging in "frolics"—began to feel deep concern for their souls.

When Jonathan spoke of the brevity and uncertainty of life and the despair of those who wait too long, there was a fervency of conviction in his voice and manner. Two young persons in the town had died suddenly in April 1734, and their companions were greatly sobered, understandably, by these deaths. Edwards the preacher seized his opportunity, and it was altogether appropriate that he do so.

At the same time Jonathan gathered together groups

of young people in his home for prayer and catechism instruction. To Jonathan, it was important that he observe their study on a firsthand basis and guide them personally on a journey toward greater piety. In the past, only the parents had assumed such responsibility, and it was inevitable that the young clergyman would incur criticism for his evangelistic actions.

Furthermore, because Jonathan hammered away at false doctrines, which had too long been a part of New England religious life, some of the more influential members of his congregation strongly opposed him as well. "We are justified by faith in Christ, and not by any manner of virtue or goodness of our own," he preached. He acknowledged that he was now throwing into jeopardy what many had been taught since their infancy, namely, that their good works, obedience, and virtue qualified them for reward. He was setting down plain biblical precepts. Some wondered if Solomon Stoddard have been wrong, or worse, could the Bible be wrong? No wonder their minds were "put into an unusual ruffle."

Jonathan's answer was to turn to God's Word. By the authority of Scripture he demonstrated the sovereignty of God, God's justice, and particularly justification by faith alone. For eight years Jonathan Edwards had lived among them but never had they heard him so eloquent and denunciatory. These themes, combined with time-honored revival methods appealing to fear and denunciation of specific sins, ignited his hearers toward an eager pursuit of salvation. The result, pure and simple, was revival.

At the same time a more modern plan of salvation loosely called Arminianism had been capturing the interest of many. Derived from the teachings of the Dutch Calvinist Jacobus Arminius (1560-1609), this new way of thinking held out hope by appealing to respectable living, being benevolent, and other virtues known as "good works." Such teachings were more comfortable than the old traditional doctrines, and it is little wonder that so many were regarding this "fashionable new divinity," as Edwards called it, with favor.

Jonathan reminded the people that God is infinite, man is finite, and the difference between the two is an infinite one. The only mediation is through Christ. Man is totally dependent on the Son of God for all his wisdom, righteousness, and redemption. Let all men who appear "eminent in holiness, and abundant in good works" hear the truth, Jonathan proclaimed: There is "an absolute and universal dependence of the redeemed on God for all their good"; and God hereby "is exalted and glorified in the work of redemption."

To this young, fiery preacher, anything less than such an attitude robbed God of His due glory and thwarted the whole plan of human redemption as God had designed it. This sermon, which came to be known as "God Glorified in Man's Dependence," included the following:

> *The doctrines I preach are living and intoxi-*
> *cating because they arise from experiential*
> *knowledge. Supreme among these doctrines is*
> *the one affirming an inscrutable, immutable*
> *Deity for adoration, not for mere speculation.*
> *Let us never forget that our relationship with the*
> *Deity, who is under no obligation to us, is at*

best a relationship of dependence, regardless of what our works and reason say to the contrary.

Two other magnificent messages showed the importance of the drama of conversion and highlighted God as the divine initiator of revelation and grace. The first was entitled "A Divine and Supernatural Light," and the other, "Justification by Faith Alone." Personal spiritual struggle accompanied Edwards's hard-won insights and the deepening meanings conveyed in these messages. There could be no doubt that this pastor meant business—spiritual business.

Relentlessly he called out the roll of sins that he proclaimed shut men out from God's mercy and kindled the divine wrath to their destruction. The townspeople's nerves were on edge, and people were beginning to cry out, "What must I do to be saved?" Religious experience seized individuals and the community alike, and soon all Northampton was caught up in what Edwards called "God's redemptive work."

Although this part of New England was a land of clergymen and small farmers, they were a vigorous, hardworking, and lusty stock of people. Women often found themselves pregnant before they were married, and special occasions were celebrated with plenty of ale, cider, and rum. Sexual virility, or the lack thereof, was a favorite subject at such bawdy gatherings. They were a quarrelsome people, going to law at the slightest provocation, and they were obstinate. Much of their religion was based on the Old Testament: They thought that if they obeyed the law of Moses well enough, Jehovah might ward off pestilences, Indians, droughts, floods, and earthquakes and reward them with good harvests. The Ten Commandments might have been memorized, but they were conveniently ignored in practice. To such a people, Jonathan Edwards's sermons must have seemed revolutionary—and devastatingly personal.

That this awakening brought an impetus for change and spiritual zeal was evident. One notable conversion occurred in December 1734, when a young woman with an unsavory reputation as being one of the "company-keepers" in the community came under conviction of her sins and sought salvation.

Like a rushing, mighty wind, the fervor took command of the community. The parsonage became busy day and night as both the saved and unsaved sought the pastor's counsel and help. Neighbor confessed faults to neighbor; "Party Strife," which had always divided Northampton, was laid aside and differences of long standing were wiped out. Jonathan Edwards had seen revivals in his father's parish as a young boy but nothing quite like this. To him it appeared to be the outpouring for which three generations of ministers had sought.

As was his custom, he captured the essence of what was taking place in a narrative entitled *A Faithful Narrative of the Surprising Work of God in the Conversion of Many Hundred Souls in Northampton and the Neighboring Towns and Villages* (1736). In this work, Jonathan chronicles the conversion of two very different persons: Abigail Hutchinson, a young, frail woman who died prematurely, and Phebe Bartlett, a child of four years old whose quest for the "things of religion" was extraordinary. In both cases, the experience of conversion was centered on emotion.

To heighten the drama of Abigail's awakening, Edwards wrote that she was a "still, quiet, reserved person" and that "there was nothing in her education that tended to enthusiasm." The narrative continues with Abigail "awakening" in the winter season "by something she heard her brother say of the necessity of being in good earnest in seeking regenerating grace." Abigail's great terror was that she had sinned against God and she felt her own prayers were of no use. Upon seeking guidance from Jonathan, her life began to turn around: "She had many extraordinary discoveries of the glory of God and Christ. . .at such and such a time, she thought she saw as much of God and had as much joy and pleasure, as was possible in this life. . . ."

Young Phebe was given to praying alone in her closet and on one occasion even told her mother that she was afraid of going to hell. After saying that, she began to cry hysterically and could not be consoled. Suddenly, Edwards writes, she "ceased crying, and began to smile, and presently said with a smiling countenance, 'Mother, the kingdom of heaven has come to me!' " From this time, he concludes, "there appeared a very remarkable abiding change in the child."

The revival reached its peak in the early spring of 1735, and in a few months Jonathan had achieved the kind of renown enjoyed by the still revered Solomon Stoddard. He was particularly proud of the number of converts, writing at one point that "three hundred souls. . .[came] to Christ in this town in the space of half a year (how many more I don't guess)." While included in this number were the very old and the very young, to Jonathan the most important group were the adolescents. To him, their behavior was regarded as an index to the state of the community. In a 1733 sermon, hc had compared the effects of true conversion to the "difference between having a rational judgment that honey is sweet, and having a sense of its sweetness."

By 1736 revivalism had spread and similar manifestations of the work of the Holy Spirit were taking place in other towns. Visitors had come to Northampton to see for themselves and then carried back favorable reports. In a short time, the revival began to bear fruit in other parishes, among them South Hadley, Suffield, Sunderland, Deerfield, Hatfield, West Springfield, Long Meadow, Enfield, Westfield, Northfield, East Windsor, Coventry, Stratford, Ripton, Tolland, Hebron, Bolton, and Woodbury.

Besides *A Faithful Narrative,* which was to become, according to Perry Miller, a "handbook" for revivals for a hundred years, in 1741, another treatise appeared bearing the title *The Distinguishing Marks of a Work of the Spirit of God, Applied to that uncommon Operation that has lately appeared on the Minds of many of the People of This Land.* And in March 1743, yet another major work was published carrying the title *Some Thoughts Concerning the present Revival of Religion in New England, And the Way in which it ought to be acknowledged and promoted.*

With the meetinghouse in Northampton filling to overflowing, the need was clearly shown for a larger facility. Accordingly, a formal vote to build was taken in November 1735, and work began in the summer of 1736. The local townsmen worked diligently and sacrificially, and the records of one Ebenezer Hunt tell the story. In March, during a crowded Sunday morning service, the gallery of the old meetinghouse had fallen, and although no one was killed, even though more than seventy persons were seated directly underneath, it was felt they were protected by the tops of the high pews, and certainly by the hand of God. True to his nature, at the next service, Jonathan had chosen for his sermon topic "Rebuke of God and a Loud Call to Repent." After all, why shouldn't God choose to speak through the decaying beams of an old building! The congregation picked themselves up, nursed their bruises, thanked the Almighty that they were alive, and eagerly awaited the dedication of the new sanctuary.

On July 21, 1737, Ebenezer Hunt's notes state that "the spire [of the new building] was raised with good success." No one had been hurt in the whole process, he wrote, and there were probably many shouts of "Hallelujah!" and "Praise be to God!" as the people watched. On the Sunday following the raising, Jonathan Edwards, with his superb feel for choosing appropriate texts, preached from Amos 9:6: "It is he that buildeth his stories in the heaven." In this scriptural analogy linking the hand of God with the work of the raisers, the raisers themselves looked at their splintered hands and realized their preacher knew what he was about.

On Christmas Day 1737, Jonathan formally dedicated the new building. His text from John 14:2 was not surprising: "In my Father's house are many mansions." It was a memorable day in his life and in the history of Northampton. His second sermon in the new place was appropriately entitled, "The Greatest Glory of an house for Publick Worship is the Presence of Christ in it." The new meetinghouse remained the outward symbol of the great early awakening ingathering. No other young preacher in all of New England had such a record of souls gathered in.

In Jonathan Edwards, the people of Northampton had a preacher who would neither surrender nor compromise to liberalism or Arminianism—whatever one chose to call it—but would faithfully obey the God he served and preach the Word of God as he understood it. He was absorbed in the high issues of eternity, always aware of the need to help people understand the brevity of life and the terrible importance of coming to grips with God and His way of salvation. And he was concerned with the hearts of all the parishioners under his care.

The results of his preaching were conviction of sin, repentance unto life, and a revival of sincere piety among those who were influenced—that there was a reawakened interest in genuine religious experience in the Christian context cannot be denied. Jonathan Edwards has been criticized for appealing to fear with his preaching, warning and urging the people to abandon their sinful practices and devote themselves to the means of salvation—Bible reading, prayer, meditation, and church attendance. Yet, while he proclaimed the anger and wrath of God in words that have survived to this day, there was always present in his spirit and words the wooing note of Christ's love and mercy.

Yet for all the power of Jonathan's revival in Northampton, when it was over, it was truly over. In the years between the awakening of 1734–35 and the Great Awakening of 1740–42, the Connecticut Valley seemed to relapse spiritually into its prerevival state. The end was signalled by the suicide of Joseph Hawley, who was married to Solomon Stoddard's daughter, Rebecca. Discouraged over the state of his soul, Hawley slit his throat on a Sabbath morning. According to Jonathan, such an act was the devil's doing: Only God's mercy has kept humanity from "adultery or sodomy or buggery or murder or blasphemy as others have done or [from having] destroyed our own lives." Jonathan went on to say, "We are all in ourselves utterly without any strength or power to help ourselves."

The Great Awakening itself was an upheaval destroying much that was good, encouraging lamentable excesses, and ushering in an era of bitterness and false charges, misrepresentations intended to blacken the reputation of others. And yet, the Great Awakening, with its extravagances and tragic mistakes, was to be considered one of the most potent and constructive forces in American life during the midcentury. A wave of spiritual distress and of a longing for Christ and His salvation appeared in the Connecticut Valley in 1740, and for sixteen to eighteen months it spread throughout the valley and into the nearby villages and towns.

What further role would Jonathan now play in this tumultuous event?

nine

For more than three years the churchgoing people of New England held high hopes that a revival to match Northampton's would take place. While there had been indications of revival in some of the villages, the movement hadn't carried itself along to meet expectations. Now, however, religious life in America was to experience an extraordinary metamorphosis. The transition from staid and sterile to emotional and passionate was nothing short of astounding.

The Great Awakening was signalled by the arrival in 1740 of a fiery evangelist named George Whitefield who landed on American soil from London, England. His arrival was preceded by letters from London ministers testifying to his powers, letters that were published in Boston papers. It is noteworthy that adverse accounts also received were omitted. Whitefield's press agent, William Seward, his "companion in travel," dealt with the press, making sure press notices were admirably calculated to keep curiosity at its zenith.

The time was ripe, however, for the Whitefield brand of evangelism and the manner in which events at his meetings took place. For too long there had been coldness and indifference in many churches, and following the success at Northampton, what was then considered America appeared on the threshold of a great revival. Throughout the colonies there were to be found preachers who were prepared. A spirit of prayer was present in various churches and in some places the people were already showing the concern for the salvation of their souls, which was to become so widespread.

History credits Whitefield with launching the Great Awakening. More than anyone else, he insisted upon the sinner's thoroughgoing dependence upon divine mercy, moving great numbers of otherwise apathetic people through persuasive oratory and mannerisms to a fresh consideration of their spiritual lives.

News spread surprisingly quickly in those days, and when Whitefield set foot in a town, he was assured of a large audience. They came, no doubt, out of some degree of curiosity, but there was also a hunger. Many New Englanders were convinced that God had selected these days for a very special outpouring of His Spirit; many supposed this to be their last chance before the arrival of the millennium. Whatever was taking place, it was mysterious and exciting, accompanied by hysteria, faintings, shriekings, and souls being added to the kingdom.

In sharp contrast to the solemn preaching to which New Englanders were accustomed, Whitefield raved, stared, beat his breast, and, in general, put on quite a pulpit and stage show affording the people some entertainment, but all with the element of religious drama.

It should be noted that New Englanders had always approved of preachers with power—powerful tones as well as powerful messages—but Whitefield was in a new category. Whatever one may think of his methods, there were those, even among some of the elite clergymen of that day, especially in Boston, who spoke favorably about him to a degree. There he spoke to five thousand on the Common and to eight thousand in the fields. And for ten days he traveled to church after church with thousands at his heels.

Whitefield was actually a beginner in things spiritual, a young man full of zest and fervor, with preaching as his one thought and desire. Success had come too early for this young evangelist-revivalist—he was only twenty-five at the time of his 1740 triumph in America. But he did leave a mark, disarming even the skeptical, and he himself said men may be used of God to do greater than they know.

So it was that Jonathan Edwards invited him to Northampton.

In a letter dated February 12, 1740, Edwards conveyed his thoughts regarding the condition in New England, which he saw as being favorable to revival. That letter reveals a warm-hearted Edwards ready for what he sensed God was about to do:

Rev. sir,
My request to you is that in your intended
journey through New England the next summer

you would be pleased to visit Northampton. I hope it is not wholly from curiosity that I desire to see and hear you in this place, but I apprehend, from what I have heard, that you are one that has the blessing of heaven attending you wherever you go, and I have a great desire, if it be the will of God, that such blessing as attends your person and labours may descend on this town. Indeed I am fearful whether you will not be disappointed in New England, and will have less success here than in other places. We who have dwelt in a land that has been distinguished with light, and have long enjoyed the Gospel, and have been glutted with it, and have despised it, are I fear more hardened than most of those places where you have preached hitherto. But yet I hope in that power and mercy of God that has appeared so triumphant in the success of your labours in other places, that he will send a blessing with you even to us, tho' we are unworthy of it. I hope, if God spares my life, to see something of that salvation of God in New England which He has now begun in a benighted, wicked and miserable world and age and in the most guilty of nations.

It has been with refreshment of soul that I have heard of one raised up in the Church of England to revive the mysterious, spiritual, despised and exploded doctrines of the Gospel, and full of a spirit of zeal for the promotion of real, vital piety, whose labours have been

*attended with such success. Blessed be God that
hath done it! who is with you, and helps you,
and makes the weapons of your warfare mighty.
We see that God is faithful and never will forget
the promises that He has made to His church,
and that He will not suffer the smoking flax to
be quenched, even when the floods seem to be
overwhelming it, but will revive the flame again,
even in the darkest times. I hope this is the
dawning of a day of God's mighty power and
glorious grace to the world of mankind. . .and
may God send forth more labourers into His
harvest of a like spirit, until the kingdom of
Satan shall shake and his proud Empire fall
throughout the earth and the kingdom of Christ,
that glorious kingdom of light, holiness, peace
and love, shall be established from one end of
the earth unto the other! . . . .*

Jonathan Edwards closed this gracious letter by explaining that "The way from New York to Boston through Northampton. . .leads through as populous a part of the country as any. . . ."

Whitefield's reputation, of course, had preceded him. According to Winslow, instead of doctrine logically stated, proved, and applied, according to a carefully prepared plan of argument, he dramatized both the biblical narrative and the application, spoke entirely without notes, made violent gestures, laughed, sang, and shed public tears. Nothing like this had ever happened in the name of religion.

After careful examination of Whitefield's sermons, which did appear in print, theologians and biographers were able to analyze and explain the man and his message. Some said that his powers "were chiefly that of the platform." Others observed that he "repeated himself endlessly." One critic outspokenly pointed out that "everything he had to say in a lifetime he said in any one sermon." The written messages "were as dull as the port-folios of ministerial dispute which they incited." But "his imagination was as agile as his body, his sensitive-ness to the mood of an audience unerring. . . . He conquered not by force of intellect (for he was not a thinker) nor by spirituality (for he was not a [deeply] spiritual man), but by the tones, the oratorical wizardry, the personal magnetism he could exert over an audience. . . ."

Miller speaks of New England being a powder keg: Jonathan Edwards had already put a match to the fuse, and George Whitefield blew it into a flame.

Jonathan Edwards reserved judgment on the man, and it is known that he eagerly anticipated Whitefield's arrival on Friday, October 17, 1740. Since he stayed as a guest at the parsonage, Jonathan had ample opportunity to observe the man. Still, to Whitefield's credit, extraor-dinarily sensitive to atmosphere as he was, it appears that he was careful in his choice of words and manner-isms in Edwards's pulpit.

Jonathan had expressed to Eleazar Wheelock that he hoped Whitefield's coming would be blessed to the good of his own soul and the souls of his people. Considering the successful awakening just a few short years before, it is perhaps surprising that Jonathan describes the scene in his parish as a "sorrowfully dull and dead time."

Whitefield later wrote of his four-day visit with the Edwards family and the Northampton meetings as being wonderfully satisfying, noting, "A sweeter couple I have not yet seen." It should be remembered that he had been traveling throughout New England for almost a month, spending his days and nights in ministers' homes, but something in the King Street home of this family called for a special remark on his part. It has been said of Whitefield that praise of others didn't come easily, so his tribute to Jonathan Edwards and his family and parish is notable.

Whitefield preached four times from the Northampton pulpit and once at the parsonage. Writing about this, Whitefield said: "We crossed the ferry to Northampton where no less than three hundred souls were saved about five years ago. . . . [Dear Mr. Edwards is] a solid, excellent Christian, but, at present, weak in body. I think, I may say I have not seen his fellow in all New England. When I came into his pulpit, I found my heart drawn out to talk of scarce anything besides the consolations and privileges of saints, and the plentiful effusion of the Spirit upon the hearts of believers. And, when I came to remind them of their former experiences, and how zealous and lively they were at that time, both minister and people wept much; and the Holy Ghost enabled me to speak with a great deal of power."

Jonathan confirms in his writings that "the congregation was extraordinarily melted by every sermon; almost the whole assembly being in tears for a great part of the sermon time. . . . Mr. Whitefield's sermons were suitable

to the circumstances of the town." Following Whitefield's visit, Jonathan felt that the spark of piety, ignited
so profoundly years earlier, had been rekindled. This
time, however, an itinerant preacher had stirred the
Northampton flock and not their own esteemed pastor.

When Whitefield left on Monday, as was his custom,
Jonathan Edwards rode with him as far as East Windsor,
where the two bade each other good-bye "with some
inward Regret." Whitefield went south through Connecticut Colony, writing a different revival story in each colony
through which he passed.

That same week Sarah Edwards wrote to her brother
in New Haven, the Reverend James Pierrepont, to tell
him about Whitefield's visit and preaching and to
encourage him to welcome the preacher. It is of interest
to see from a woman's view the effect of Whitefield's
messages. Plainly, God was at work:

> *It is wonderful to see what a spell he casts
> over an audience by proclaiming the simplest
> truths of the Bible. I have seen upwards of a
> thousand people hang on his words with breath-
> less silence, broken only by an occasional half-
> suppressed sob. He impresses the ignorant, and
> not less the educated and refined. It is reported
> that while the miners of England listened to
> him, the tears made white furrows down their
> smutty cheeks. So here, our mechanics shut up
> their shops, and the day-labourers throw down
> their tools, to go and hear him preach, and few
> return unaffected. . . . He speaks from a heart*

*all aglow with love, and pours out a torrent of
eloquence which is almost irresistible. Many,
very many persons in Northampton date the
beginning of new thoughts, new desires, new
purposes, and a new life, from the day on which
they heard him preach of Christ and this salvation. Perhaps I ought to tell you that Mr.
Edwards and some others think him in error on
a few practical points; but his influence on the
whole is so good we ought to bear with little
mistakes.*

The record of a farmer, Nathan Cole, also provides
some idea both of the interest that was kindled in spiritual things and of the way large congregations would
gather with very little advance notice:

*Now it pleased God to send Mr. Whitefield
into this land and my hearing of his preaching at
Philadelphia, like one of the old apostles, and
many thousands flocking after him to hear the
gospel and great numbers converted to Christ, I
felt the Spirit of God drawing me by conviction.
. . . Next I heard he was on Long Island and next
at Boston and next at Northampton and then,
one morning, all of a sudden, about 8 or 9
o'clock there came a messenger and said, 'Mr.
Whitefield preached at Hartford and Wethersfield
yesterday and is to preach at Middletown this
morning at 10 o'clock.' I was in my field, at
work, I dropped my tool that I had in my hand*

and ran home and ran through my house and bade my wife get ready quick to go and hear Mr. Whitefield preach at Middletown and ran to my pasture for my horse with all my might, fearing I should be too late to hear him. I brought my horse home and soon mounted and took my wife up and went forward as fast as I thought the horse could bear, and when my horse began to be out of breath I would get down and put my wife in the saddle and bid her ride as fast as she could and not stop or slack for me except I bade her, and so I would run until I was almost out of breath and then mount my horse again, and so I several times to favour my horse. . .for we had twelve miles to ride double in little more than an hour.

    On high ground I saw before me a cloud of fog rising, I first thought off from the great river but as I came nearer the road I heard a noise something like a low rumbling of horses feet coming down the road and this cloud was a cloud of dust made by the running of horses' feet. It arose some rods in the air, over the tops of the hills and trees, and when I came within about twenty rods of the road I could see men and horses slipping along in the cloud like shadows and when I came nearer it was like a steady stream of horses and their riders, scarcely a horse more than his length behind another, all of a lather and some with sweat. . . .

*We went down with the stream, I heard no
man speak a word all the way, three miles, but
everyone pressing forward in great haste, and
when we got down to the old meetinghouse
there was a great multitude—it was said to be
3 or 4,000 people assembled together. We got
off from our horses and shook off the dust, and
the ministers were then coming to the meetinghouse. I turned and looked towards the great
river and saw ferry boats running swift, forward and backward, bringing over loads of
people, the oars rowed nimble and quick.
Everything, men, horses and boats, all seemed
to be struggling for life, the land and the banks
over the river looked black with people and
horses. All along the 12 miles I saw no man at
work in his field but all seemed to be gone.*

Writing about what happened at this Wethersfield meeting, a townsperson reported to a friend, "The whole town seemed shaken. . . . Last Monday night the Lord bowed the heavens and came down upon a large assembly in one of the parishes in the town, the whole assembly seemed alive with distress, the groans and outcries of the wounded were such that my voice could not be heard."

And this was at the beginning of the revival! Accounts like this traveled far and wide, accounting in part for the enormous crowds that surged to the Whitefield meetings wherever they were held.

Those who stood at the very center of events of that time were persuaded that success was not in the hands of mere man to bestow. Unitedly they felt with new force the words of Christ: "The wind bloweth where it listeth, and thou hearest the sound thereof, but canst not tell whence it cometh, and whither it goeth" (John 3:8).

In an article entitled "Evangelism of the Eighteenth Century," in *The British and Foreign Evangelical Review*, published in January 1862, it was stated that one of the prominent features of the Great Awakening was that the Gospel was armed by the Holy Spirit with a tremendous and irresistible *individualizing* power. "Man was made to come forth into the light and take his appropriate place before God as guilty and accountable."

Murray explains that the nature of the preaching in the Great Awakening was often alarming, and intentionally so. The preachers knew that the absence of fear was ruining man from one generation to another. But they also believed that neither they nor even the truth itself could induce the fear that leads to life eternal. Only a *consciousness* of the presence of God could make the truths preached startlingly real to preachers and hearers alike. Then the fact of final judgment could be no more doubted than if it were already present. What one young person said of Jonathan Edwards's preaching in 1739 was equally true of the speeches of others at this time: "I fully supposed that as soon as Mr. Edwards should close his discourse, the Judge would descend and the final separation take place."

The Great Awakening was over. What was now needed in the villages of New England was sound guidance. And Jonathan Edwards was prepared to provide it.

ten

Jonathan Edwards had warned from the beginning of the revival movement that dangerous excesses would be likely to appear during the Great Awakening. When Edwards met privately with Whitefield on his Northampton visit, he presented to him the need for not relying too much upon impulse in religion. Later, Edwards was to publicly recommend due caution. Still, he was willing to consider that the errors and excesses were accidental effects and that the Awakening was essentially a work of the Holy Spirit. To that end, he cooperated in the follow-up work with his own powerful preaching.

Edwards hated lukewarm religion, but he also saw and recognized that religious "experience" is never wholly pure or free from the "natural and carnal." Natural passion can get out of control and faintings, tears, groans, agonizing outcries, and bodily tremors—all observed at gatherings during the Great Awakening—can be disruptive and

89

also lead to spiritual pride. Still, Edwards defended revivalism even though he had no illusions about man's immoderate tendencies.

Edwards knew the Word of God. He was familiar with the prophet Jeremiah's outcry, expressing the anguish and agony of heart of that prophet (Jeremiah 4:19), and that of other Old Testament prophets who experienced bodily effects as God dealt with their hearts; twenty years earlier, he himself had experienced a quickening and awakening. He would not discount that God works in men's lives in different ways.

Miller observes that Jonathan Edwards "was at the height of his career and influence" at this juncture in his life. Because he refused to participate in attacking the Awakening, as many in the religious community were then doing, he became established in the mind of the public as the foremost spokesman for the pro-Awakening forces.

The next chapter in the movement was to take place as Jonathan Edwards preached at a revival in Enfield, Massachusetts, on July 8, 1741. It was a rural congregation, and Edwards was a last-minute substitute for the guest speaker. He had arrived on horseback with a sermon in his pocket, prepared as always for any situation that might arise. But the sermon he would give this day was unique. In fact, many historians agree that no other sermon preached in America has received comparable attention.

All revival meetings at that time carried with them the expectation that the theme of the speaker would be in keeping with the newest revival emphasis or the wrath of

God and the imminence of everlasting punishment. People were talking about the end times, which proved the best of times for Jonathan Edwards's pulpit oratory as he had a peculiar power in delivering messages on this subject.

He took as his text Deuteronomy 32:35: "Their foot shall slide in due time." In reporting on this, Wheelock mentions how the people, whom he characterized as "thoughtless and vain," were so enchanted before the sermon was ended that they were "bowed down with an awful conviction of their sin and danger."

Stephen Williams, another eyewitness, wrote an account of what happened the same day in his diary:

> *Before sermon was done—there was a great moaning and crying out through ye whole House—What Shall I do to be savd—oh I am going to Hell—Oh what shall I do for Christ & c. So yet ye minister was obliged to desist—ye shrieks & crys were piercing & Amazing—after Some time of waiting the Congregation were Still so yet a prayer was made by Mr. W. & after that we descended from the pulpitt and discoursed with the people—Some in one place and Some in another—and Amazing and Astonishing ye power God was seen - & Several Souls were hopefully wrought upon yt night, & oh ye cheerfulness and pleasantness of their countenances yt receivd comfort. . . .*

It has been said, mistakenly, that the Enfield sermon

was a description of hell. Rather, Edwards's text concerned the time between the present and one's death, an unknown quantity. Death comes suddenly and unannounced, as Edwards showed in these memorable words:

> *The unseen, unthought of ways and means of persons' going suddenly out of the world are innumerable and inconceivable. Unconverted men walk over the pit of hell on a rotten covering, and there are innumerable places in this covering so weak that they will not bear their weight, and these places are not seen. The arrows of death fly unseen at noonday; the sharpest sight cannot discern them.*

The imagery he used was deliberate in design, intended to communicate the sense of a disaster near at hand.

> *There are the black clouds of God's wrath now hanging directly over your heads, full of the dreadful storm, and big with thunder; and were it not for the restraining hand of God, it would immediately burst upon you. The sovereign pleasure of God, for the present, stays His rough wind: otherwise it would come with fury, and your destruction would come like a whirlwind, and you would be like the chaff of the summer threshing floor.*

Then he turns from imagery to making it personal for each person seated before him.

There is reason to think that there are many in this congregation now hearing this discourse, that will actually be the subjects of this very misery to all eternity. We know not who they are, or in what seats they sit, or what thoughts they now have. It may be they are now at ease, and hear all these things without much disturbance, and are now flattering themselves that they are not the persons; promising themselves that they shall escape. . . . But alas!. . .how many is it likely will remember this discourse in hell! And it would be a wonder, if some that are now present would not be in hell in a very short time, before this year is out. And it would be no wonder if some persons, that now sit here in some seats of this meeting-house in health, and quiet and secure, should be there before tomorrow morning.

God was angry, Jonathan Edwards propounded, and nothing but God's own hand held Him back. He allowed divine wrath to stand unrelieved.

The purpose of this kind of preaching is clear enough and can be summarized in Edwards's own statement: "The only opportunity of escaping is in this world; this is the only state of trial wherein we have any offers of mercy, or there is any place for repentance."

The message is for all time: With death each person loses the opportunity to change the final balance of his life. After death there is no hope whatsoever. The torments of hell are eternal. God is omnipotent, God is angry, and man is wholly lost without recognizing his condition and turning to Him.

These were, in fact, the pillars sustaining the structure of Jonathan Edwards's theology. This was not just Calvinist doctrine, as some detractors have interpreted. The essential point he sought to declare emphatically was that hell is inseparable from religious experience and that to know salvation is first to know the darkness of alienation from God.

For all his eloquence, perhaps Jonathan had a simple purpose in preaching "Sinners in the Hands of an Angry God": He wanted his listeners to envision with him the heaven promised by the saving Gospel. And he wanted them to understand the nature of true religion.

eleven

Despite the Great Awakening, many congregations and their pastors alike lacked spiritual vitality. George Whitefield, upon returning to England, summarized the situation in these words: "I am greatly persuaded that the generality of preachers talk of an unknown, unfelt Christ. And the reason why congregations have been so dead is because dead men preach to them."

Such was not the case with the Reverend Jonathan Edwards, who viewed his work as a minister of the Gospel to speak to men in the name of God, calling them to recognize their need to know God personally. The first demand, however, in his calling, was that his own knowledge of God should be firsthand. His whole ministry was based upon the conviction that the usefulness of his work was related to the nature of his inner life. Personal communion with God came first, and it was to that end that he maintained daily set times for prayer, solitude, meditation, and earnest study—thirteen hours, every day. His study was itself a sanctuary, and whether he was wrestling with Scripture or preparing sermons or writing in his notebooks, he worked as a worshiper. He knew what he wished to preach, and he took great pains and time to write out what he meant so that his hearers might be affected and moved to action. Much meditation and writing preceded his preaching. Turnbull points out that there is in the sermons a method of structure with unfailing regularity and sometimes without flaw. Divisions are named, points under each one are numbered, and objections are presented and answered. Clarity marks the work of Edwards: He knew that the plain man was reached best by the plain style.

Jonathan Edwards set high and exacting standards for himself, and he had come to see that the main "business" of the ministry was to expound the living Word of God. He wrote, "The work and business of ministers of the Gospel is as it were that of servants, to wash and cleanse the souls of men; for this is done by preaching of the Word, which is their main business: Ephesians 5:26—'That he might sanctify and cleanse it with the washing of water by the word'." He felt he was a steward of the truth and that he must be diligent and faithful so that the conscience of the people would be cleansed. He spoke of the ministry of the Gospel as "a great work."

The very nature of redemptive Christianity means that Christians are to be people of prayer. "Seeing we have such a prayer-hearing God as we have," he told his people, "let us all be much employed in the duty of prayer, let us live prayerful lives, continuing instant in prayer." He expanded on this topic, once again invoking Scripture:

> *Christ Himself, though the eternal Son of God, obtained the Holy Spirit for Himself in a way of prayer. Luke 3:21, 22, "Jesus also being baptized, and praying, the heaven was opened, and the Holy Ghost descended. . .like a dove upon him." If we have the Spirit of God dwelling in us, we shall have Christ Himself thereby living in us. . . . If that fountain of light dwells richly in us, we shall shine like Him.*

In another sermon, based on John 5:35—"He was a burning and a shining light"— he wrote:

> *In order to this, ministers should be diligent in their studies, and in the work of the ministry; giving themselves wholly to it. . . . And particularly, ministers should be very conversant with the Holy Scriptures, they are the light by which ministers should be enlightened and they are the fire whence their hearts and the hearts of their hearers must be kindled.*

Edwards argued that it is through intimacy with heaven that men are made "great blessings in the world." Referring to Moses and the Apostle Paul, he wrote, ". . .if we in good earnest apply ourselves. . .we may come with boldness, and converse with God as a friend." Throughout his writings there is an emphasis upon the need "to be much in seeking the influences of His Spirit." He expressed his longing for Spirit-anointed preaching "which alone can revive the church and awaken the world." It was this style that would address the consciences of men.

Perhaps one reason contributing to the spiritual apathy following the Great Awakening was the continued and heated debate among New England theologians concerning that dramatic period of revival. Jonathan Edwards's clear-cut logic, his precision of phrase, and his tenacity in presentation, seeking to exonerate Whitefield from false charges, placed him in a difficult position with many leaders in the clergy and his alma mater, Yale. (From that time on, he attended Princeton's commencements instead of Yale's.)

The Great Awakening and its aftermath became the subject of a series of sermons preached by Jonathan in 1744, sermons that were later preserved in Edwards's *Treatise Concerning Religious Affections* (1746). His assessment of New England's needs and the effects of the revival fires were widely read. "An intemperate, imprudent zeal, and a degree of enthusiasm, soon crept in and mingled itself with that revival of religion; and so great and general an awakening being quite a new thing in the land, at least as to all the living inhabitants of it, neither people nor ministers had learned thoroughly to *distinguish* between solid religion and its delusive counterfeits. Even many ministers of the Gospel, of long standing and the best reputation, were for a time overpowered with the glaring appearance of the latter."

Despite his now secure reputation as a "fire and

brimstone" preacher, to be moved by strong emotions, Edwards wrote, cannot necessarily be considered religious. Thus, *Religious Affections* addressed in particular the question, What is the nature of true religion? As David Levin has written, "None but a man of remarkable poise of judgment could have written it. It betrays no reaction against the movement [the Great Awakening] which had come short of what he hoped."

Because Edwards always sought just the right word in his writings, there is an exactness and vividness in his use of language in *Religious Affections*. In this treatise he provides a magnificent comparison between true saints and those merely puffed up by the experience of vigorous but fleeting emotions. Hypocrites are likened to meteors that flare up suddenly in a blaze of light, trailing showers of many sparks, but soon fall back to earth, their light dissipated. True saints, however, are like the fixed stars; they shine by a light that is steady and sure, a light that continues to show itself over time and through the infinite spaces.

The excesses of emotionalism that the revival had produced in some, including bodily effects, are not signs that men are truly religious. Edwards didn't say that bodily effects can't occur, but rather, the emphasis involves a "new spiritual sense." This is what true Christian affections are all about. This involves more specifically a new attitude of the heart toward God; an unselfish love for divine things because they are holy; a spiritual enlightenment that leads to a conviction of the certainty of divine truth and a humiliating sense of unworthiness. It shows itself by a change of disposition that manifests love, meekness, tenderness of spirit, and a life of real Christian conduct in our relations to others. And it all happens by the indwelling of the Holy Spirit.

A merely nodding of one's head to Christianity is inadequate. It leaves the individual outside as a spectator looking in on a feast; what is needed instead is an engagement of the self and the inclination of the heart and will. In *Religious Affections* Jonathan took great pains to center attention on the gracious activity of the Spirit in the *individual* soul, which establishes the genuine religious life.

The "approval of the godly" was seen by many Puritans as a criterion for judging affections. Edwards's contention was and is of utmost importance: External judgment, that is, the judgment of one man upon another, is not only unreliable but ultimately impossible. The saints, though they know "experimentally" what true religion is in their own selves, have no power of discerning the *heart* of another. He cited 1 Samuel 16:7 as his authority: "The Lord seeth not as man seeth; for man looketh on the outward appearance, but the Lord looketh on the heart."

The contemporary relevance of *Religious Affections* can readily be seen in the earnestness of Edwards's masterful treatment of a basic theological problem. The Holy Spirit is involved in the Christian's life and not in a tomb! Religion has to do with the inner nature of man, with the treasure on which his heart is set and with the love, the *affections*, that supplies his life with purpose. Beware of fleeting emotions and from the effects wrought by the rhetoric of an hour. Edwards's calm words in the midst of "much noise about religion," both for his time and the present age, is that religion is lifeless if it is based only on doctrine and good conduct. His sobering caution to revivalists in any generation was drawn from the Bible, expressed in this paraphrase: "Test the affections to see whether they are from God, for many false affections have gone out into the earth."

What was needed was leadership by men of balanced judgment, and that is what Jonathan Edwards sought to provide. He didn't discredit what had happened during the Great Awakening revivals; a sufficient explanation was human weakness. His plea was to let criticism cease and to let the glory of God be exalted by righteous conduct.

But these issues were only part of what made *Religious Affections* so controversial. In an attempt to mold his flock once again into a pious, level-headed group, one not dominated by excessive emotions, Jonathan took his first public stand against a long-standing practice of the Stoddard era. Further study had persuaded him that the town's practice of admitting to the church anyone who desired was wrong. The early Puritans were right, Jonathan declared, and true Christian practice should restrict full church membership to those able to make a profession of faith and give evidence of their conversion.

What began as a treatise on religion quickly became a discourse on the role of Jonathan Edwards in Northampton. To Jonathan, imbued with Timothy Edwards's notion of absolute authority, not to mention the overwhelming success of the first awakening, his flock had no choice but to follow his lead.

For the esteemed preacher, there would be no balm in Northampton.

twelve

Northampton had long savored its liberal reputation and its historic connection with the legendary Solomon Stoddard. Now Jonathan Edwards, from the pulpit and on paper, had dared to challenge his own grandfather's memory! Furthermore, he was throwing out the Half-Way Covenant used in almost all the churches of New England. From 1744 until 1748 the issue of church membership smoldered, as not a single applicant presented himself as a prospective candidate.

But perhaps just as damaging to Jonathan's pastorate was what came to be known as the "bad books" incident of 1744. A handbook for midwives was discovered to be circulating among the youth of the community, a book replete with graphic diagrams that were irresistible to many adolescent boys. Reading the book was bad enough, but the boys then began to taunt the girls, calling them "nasty creatures" and so on.

It has been noted that Jonathan and Sarah had a heart for the needs of young people in their midst. However, Jonathan was not timid when addressing the errors of the youth. In this instance, upon hearing about such behavior, Jonathan handled the situation in his usual pious way. One Sunday following the service he stated the particulars of the incident to the congregation and asked the parishioners to elect a committee of inquiry. For some reason, at the same time he also read the names of those youngsters involved and the witnesses who had identified who was whom. The custom in those days in church life was to expose such problems, even those as trivial as someone not paying his bills promptly. Families were humiliated publicly as parish critics and troublemakers pounced on things that were actually none of their business. Parish problems were thus shared by the whole community as almost all of the families were attached to the congregation. While this entire scenario was likely mismanaged, the result was nothing short of tragic: The young people and their families and friends became irrevocably set against Jonathan Edwards.

According to Samuel Hopkins, Jonathan's dear friend, the bad books incident caused the town to be "all in a blaze." Hopkins concluded that Edwards "greatly lost his influence" with the young people and the town as a whole. In forcing the issue—by demanding an inquiry and exposing the youngsters publicly—Jonathan provided an opportunity for the young and old of Northampton to show their disrespect openly for the one in the pulpit.

Emotions remained at a simmer when Jonathan preached on "Joseph's Temptation" after learning that young people in the community were practicing "bundling," that is, sleeping or lying as lovers, on the same bed without undressing. Bundling was a custom that came into being because of the lack of privacy in large families with small houses, or at least such was the way the townspeople explained it. These parish families had overlooked, according to Edwards, that which "leads and exposes to sin." To Northampton's fearless minister, if holiness and wholesomeness of life would redeem the community, it would come when "the dross of base desire was scorched away in the love of God."

Jonathan cared deeply for the families under him and he was concerned for the moral state of the town of Northampton. Social conditions were not utopian in the commonwealth of New England, explains Turnbull. In nearby Boston, the liquor traffic had its grip upon society with the attendant intemperance and debauchery. Slave trade was still widely prevalent. Immorality was common. A seasoned traveler, Jonathan was aware of what was going on in the colonial culture, and in the New England townships, and the contemporary events of that era. His preaching aimed in part to arouse a lethargic church to take its place as "salt" and "light" in the world. Edwards did have a sociological conscience that showed itself in pastoral concern.

Such a time of unpleasantness involved money troubles as well, and back-door gossip was directed at private affairs of the parsonage. To be sure, Jonathan was well paid for his profession and era. But every year, when he would receive his annual grant, there would be contentious bickering and embarrassing inquiries into his and Sarah's spending habits. Finally, in March 1748, Jonathan and the church eventually agreed on a fixed wage, a sum that nonetheless was negotiated anew each year.

Even after twenty years in the pulpit, the Reverend Mr. Edwards hadn't learned much about the delicacy of human relations. Through it all, Jonathan Edwards walked quite alone, clinging tenaciously to the plane on which his own inner life was lived as revealed in *Religious Affections*.

Jonathan's difficulties in the pulpit were compounded as well by a great sadness in his family. David Brainerd, missionary to the Indians and a dear "brother" in the Lord to Jonathan who was betrothed to Jerusha Edwards, lay dying from tuberculosis at the King Street parsonage. Although Dr. Mather, the town physician, had done all he could, still the Edwards family hoped for a cure. Jerusha, in pitiful ignorance of the risk she incurred, nursed her fiance right up until his death on October 9, 1747. On that sad day, as Edwards surveyed the empty bedroom and the manuscripts Brainerd had entrusted to his care, he could affirm with the friend whose unexpected stay had brought him so much spiritual enrichment and encouragement: "I have learned, in a measure, that all good things, relating both to time and eternity, come from God."

Four months later Jerusha, too, was gone. She was only seventeen years of age, and in her father's words, "generally esteemed the Flower of the Family." It was the first break in the family circle, and it was heartbreaking even though Jonathan, his wife, and family knew both their beloved daughter and David were with the Lord.

Jonathan Edwards referred to Jerusha as "My own dear Child," and expressed how he, his wife, and Jerusha's brothers and sisters were so appreciative of the sympathy received from his people. His closing exhortation at her memorial service was directed to the young people in his church. Now there were two new graves in the family plot at the Bridge Street Cemetery.

Following Brainerd's death, Jonathan took upon himself the editing of the young missionary's voluminous diaries. *The Life of Rev. David Brainerd,* the finished product, was a publishing success, making the name of David Brainerd, missionary to "savage" Indians, better known to the average Christian in future generations than the name of Jonathan Edwards.

Jonathan understood that such professional and personal crises were inevitable. He took pains, however, to explain that "a work of God without stumbling-blocks is never to be expected." He recognized and spoke out about the devil's tactics in introducing excess and confusion into a work of God, and that "unseen warfare" was taking place.

Among the stumbling blocks Jonathan faced at this juncture, none was more overwhelming than the death on June 19, 1748, of Colonel John Stoddard. Not only was he Northampton's leading citizen and Solomon Stoddard's son, the colonel was also Jonathan's unfailing friend and uncle. A Harvard graduate and a career soldier, Stoddard had been commander-in-chief of the western Massachusetts frontier by 1744. Besides his military career, he was one of the richest men in the colony, having acquired his wealth through speculative land deals.

As long as "Uncle John" was around, there was no open criticism of the man in the pulpit. Jonathan and his wife held the colonel in such esteem that when he lay seriously ill in Boston in June, Sarah was immediately sent there to assist in his care. This left Jonathan with the care of thirteen-month-old baby Elizabeth and the rest of his children. A letter from Jonathan to his wife at that time shows him to be a father well acquainted with household affairs and grateful for the help of a Mrs. Phelps and a Hannah Root, more than likely women from his church. In his sermon at his uncle's funeral entitled "A Strong Rod Broken and Withered," Jonathan said, "Perhaps never was there a man that appeared in New England to whom the denomination of *a great man* did more properly belong. . . . He was a most faithful friend. . . ."

Now many remaining relatives—of whom there were a vast number, notably the Williams clan (four prominent clergymen)—were openly hostile to Jonathan Edwards. Edwards's aunt Rebecca, widowed by the suicide of her husband in 1735, and her son, Joseph Jr., began to attack their relative, who was also their pastor. Amazingly, four years later, young Joseph wrote a lengthy letter in which he apologized, declaring in part, "I was not only under the common obligations of each individual of the society to him, as a most able, diligent, and faithful pastor, but I had also received many instances of his tenderness, goodness and generosity to me as a young kinsman, whom he was disposed to treat in a most friendly manner." But at the time, shortly after Colonel Stoddard's death, these people and another man, Seth Pomeroy, led in the opposition to Jonathan Edwards's ministry.

The Hawleys had another reason to oppose their relative in the pulpit. In 1747 a young woman named Martha Root claimed that her illegitimate child had been sired by Lieutenant Elisha Hawley, son of Rebecca and Joseph and Jonathan's first cousin. By mid-1748, however, the Hawley and Root families had settled the matter privately, and money for the child's support had changed hands. However, soon after Jonathan interfered. To him, the preservation of human society was at stake, and he demanded that Elisha marry Martha. As perhaps another sign that his converts had deserted him, the marriage did not take place and Jonathan's support was weakened considerably.

Finally, the controversial theological issue that had begun to be addressed years earlier reared its ugly head, causing permanent damage to Jonathan's already tenuous position. Writing in *Religious Affections,* Jonathan had severed himself from Solomon Stoddard's liberal stranglehold by offering his own, conservative view of church membership. Now, as if pouring fuel onto the fire of discontent, Jonathan spoke out in his own bold way against his grandfather's open invitation to the communion table. For some time Jonathan had been keeping up a correspondence with John Erskine in Scotland (having mainly to do with advancing mission work among the Indians). He found the communion of saints to be international, and it provided consolation and encouragement to him. In one of those letters, dated May 20, 1749, he wrote: "A very great difficulty has arisen between my people, relating to qualifications for communion at the Lord's table. My honoured grandfather Stoddard, my predecessor in the ministry over this church, strenuously maintained the Lord's Supper to be a *converting ordinance*, and urged all to come who were not of scandalous life, though they knew themselves to be unconverted. I formerly conformed to his practice but I have had difficulties with respect to it, which have been long increasing, till I dared no longer to proceed in the former way, which has occasioned great uneasiness among my people, and has filled all the country with noise."

In an attempt to purify the ministry, Edwards had invited mutiny. His plea all along had been for visible evidence of godliness in communicants (those who wanted to partake of communion). Edwards's great-grandson, writing many years later about the events precipitating the dismissal, states, "The lax mode of admitting members into the church had prevailed about forty-five years, and though both Mr. Stoddard [Solomon Stoddard, Jonathan's grandfather] and Mr. Edwards had been most desirous of the prevalence of vital religion in the church, yet, a wide door having been thrown open for the admission of unconverted members, *as such,* it cannot but have been the fact, that, during this long period, many unconverted members should, through that door, have actually obtained admission into the church. . . . The consequences of Mr. Stoddard's error fell with all their weight on *his own grandson.*"

Edwards had come to the firm conviction that a wrong principle of admission to the Lord's Table imperils the whole nature of the church, for then the world and the church cease to be distinguished. He acted on that conviction. A man has to live with his conscience and he chose to adhere to scriptural truth.

Jonathan asked for permission to explain from the pulpit the reason for his change of mind, but this was denied. He then asked for the church to withhold a decision until he could prepare his reasons in written form, and he immediately began what was to become another book. All he asked for was a "fair hearing," but such was not to be the case.

The book was published with a typically "Edwardsean" title: *An Humble Inquiry into the Rules of the Word of God concerning the Qualifications requisite to a Complete Standing and Full Communion in the Visible Christian Church.* Unfortunately, and not totally unexpectedly, the book didn't get read by his church people. In the preface he wrote, "I can truly say it is what I engage in with the greatest reluctance that ever I undertook any public service in my life. . . . I am conscious, not only is the interest of religion concerned in this affair, but my own reputation, future usefulness, and my very subsistence, all seem to depend on my freely opening and defending myself, as to my principles. . . ."

The controversy raged with many efforts put forth to resolve the issues, including five public lectures. Interestingly, the aggrieved portion of the church membership stayed away, thus successfully helping to defeat the purpose of the lectures. On the surface, the primary dispute concerned the basis of admission to the sacrament of the Lord's Supper, but it went beyond that. The Northampton dismissal had many parallels in other villages in the midcentury. To some degree Edwards was the victim of a community feud that had been festering for years, and he was also a victim of the unrest that existed

111

between clergy and laity over the matter of authority. Ministerial autocracy was common throughout the early colonies and would remain an issue until after the Revolutionary War. Things were changing and the people wanted to take things more into their own hands.

The case of the pastor versus the congregation was deadlocked, and the crisis demanded that a Council of Churches be called. Such a council had to be called and convened to settle matters within local churches according to the provisions of the Cambridge Platform, on which the practice of Massachusetts churches was based. Edwards pleaded with this council, but after many meetings they went against him, and on June 22, 1750, the church voted for his dismissal. As Jonathan later recalled, "Nothing would quiet 'em till they could see the Town clear of Root & Branch, Name and Remnant."

Jonathan Edwards had just ten days to prepare his farewell sermon to the Northampton congregation. Many questions must have cycled through his thinking. There was nothing more to lose, and the future stretched before him as a blank slate.

On Sunday, July 2, 1750, as Jonathan made his way to the pulpit, all eyes were undoubtedly riveted on the renowned and maligned pastor. From time to time the parishioners likely cast their glances toward the Edwards pew, where Mrs. Edwards sat with her brood of children, one in her arms, their third son, Pierrepont, just three months old. How was the Reverend Mr. Edwards going to support himself and that large family? The whole village had become a part of all that had taken place for so many months and no one would have been able to keep aloof.

"Mr. Edwards" was now going to have the last word. He was noted for his plain speaking. If either his friends or his enemies had ventured a guess as to what he would say, Winslow says, "They were probably wrong. But few who heard would ever forget."

thirteen

Tall and erect, with Bible in hand, Jonathan Edwards stood before more than seven hundred people—the members of his congregation. It was his last and best chance for drama. He could seize the moment and publicly disgrace his accusers. He could berate his flock for disloyalty. He could make himself appear to be a martyr for righteousness' sake. He could indulge in sentimental reminiscences. Acknowledged as having a genius for always choosing appropriate Scriptures, whatever the occasion, Jonathan would not let this day be the exception.

"For our rejoicing is this, the testimony of our conscience, that in simplicity and godly sincerity, not with fleshly wisdom, but by the grace of God, we have had our conversation in the world, and more abundantly to you-ward. . . . As also ye have acknowledged us in part, that we are your rejoicing, even as ye also are our's in the day of the Lord Jesus" (2 Corinthians 1:12, 14).

115

Then he gave the statement of the *Doctrine:* "Ministers, and the people that have been under their care, must meet one another before Christ's tribunal at the day of judgment." He set the tone. The issue between himself and his flock was up to God. He had chosen to direct the thoughts of his people to that far future when each would answer before God.

> *How often have we met together in the house of God in this relation? How often have I spoke to you, instructed, counselled, warned, directed, and fed you, and administered ordinances among you, as the people which were committed to my care, and of whose precious souls I had the charge? But in all probability, this never will be again. . . .*
>
> *It was three and twenty years, the 15th day of last February, since I have laboured in the work of the ministry, in the relation of a pastor to this church and congregation. . . .*
>
> *I have spent the prime of my life and strength in labours for your eternal welfare. You are my witnesses that what strength I have had, I have not neglected in idleness, nor laid out in prosecuting worldly schemes, and managing temporal affairs, for the advancement of my outward estate and aggrandizing myself and my family; but have given myself to the work of the ministry, labouring in it night and day, rising early and applying myself to this great business to which Christ has appointed me.*

*How exceeding beautiful, and how con-
ducive to the adorning and happiness of the
town, if the young people could be persuaded,
when they meet together, to converse as
Christians and as the children of God. This is
what I have longed for: and it has been exceedingly grievous to me when I have heard of vice,
vanity and disorder among our youth. And so
far as I know my heart, it was from hence that I
formerly led this church to some measures, for
the suppressing of vice among our young people, which gave so great offence and by which I
became so obnoxious. . . .*

*I have found the work of the ministry among
you to be a great work indeed, a work of
exceeding care, labour, and difficulty. . . .*

*But now I have reason to think my work is
finished which I had to do as your minister. You
have publicly rejected me and my opportunities
cease. . .*

*A contentious people will be a miserable
people. The contentions which have been among
you, since I first became your pastor, have been
one of the greatest burdens I have laboured
under in the course of my ministry—not only the
contentions you have had with me, but those
which you have had one with another, about
your lands and other concerns—because I knew
that contention, heat of spirit, evil speaking, and
things of the like nature, were directly contrary
to the spirit of Christianity and did, in a peculiar*

manner, tend to drive away God's Spirit from a people. . .

Let the late contention about the terms of Christian communion, as it has been the greatest, be the last. I would, now I am preaching my farewell sermon, say to you, as the apostle to the Corinthians, "Finally, brethren, farewell. Be perfect, be of one mind, live in peace; and the God of love and peace shall be with you.". . .

May God bless you with a faithful pastor, one that is well acquainted with his mind and will, thoroughly warning sinners, wisely and skillfully searching professors and conducting you in the way to eternal blessedness. . . .

I desire that I may never forget this people, who have been so long my special charge, and that I may never cease to pray fervently for your prosperity. . . .

And let me be remembered in the prayers of all God's people that are of a calm spirit, and are peaceable and faithful in Israel, of whatever opinion they may be with respect to terms of church communion. And let us all remember, and never forget our future solemn meeting on that great day of the Lord; the day of infallible decision, and of the everlasting and unalterable sentence. Amen.

When he was still but a young Christian, Jonathan Edwards had prayed for patience and gentleness. One of the traits he so admired in his future wife in 1723 was her "wonderful calmness of mind." And now that calmness shone in Edwards. This was his last official duty to his flock and it was *their* needs, rather than his own, which were uppermost in his mind.

It is safe to presume that many of the people made their way sadly home that summer morning. Edwards himself later reported that many in the congregation "seemed to be much affected, and some are exceedingly grieved. Some few, I believe, have some relentings of heart that [they] voted me away."

Five days later he wrote to William M'Culloch in Scotland: "I am now departed from the people between whom and me there was once the greatest union. Remarkable is the providence of God in this matter. In this event we have a striking instance of the instability and uncertainty of all things here below."

As the days progressed into weeks, and then months, uncertainty about his future and that of his family became more pronounced. Jonathan must have reminded Sarah, as well as himself, of the overruling providence of God. It was a difficult situation he faced, a situation that would be bolstered by his strong faith. In the midst of anxiety about the future and very real sorrow at leaving Northampton and their home, he prayed to God for an open door of usefulness.

From his own "Journal on the Communion Controversy," Jonathan wrote, "A minister by his office is to be the guide and instructor of his people. To that end he is to study and search the Scriptures and to teach the people, not the opinions of men—of other divines or of their ancestors—but the mind of Christ. As he is set to enlighten them, so a part of his duty is to rectify their mistakes, and, if he sees them out of the way of truth or duty, to be a voice behind them saying, 'This is the way, walk ye in it.' Hence, if what he offers to exhibit to them as the mind of Christ be different from their previous apprehensions, unless it be on some point which is established in the Church of God as fundamental, surely they are obliged to hear him. If not, there is an end at once to all the use and benefit of teachers in the church in these respects—as the means of increasing its light and knowledge, and of reclaiming it from mistakes and errors. This would be in effect to establish, not the word of Christ, but the opinion of the last generation in each town and church, as an immutable rule to all future generations to the end of the world."

Four days after his farewell sermon, he wrote to his Scottish friend John Erskine, "I am now, as it were, thrown upon the wide ocean of the world, and know not what will become of me and my numerous and chargeable family. Nor have I any particular door in view that I depend upon to be opened for my future serviceableness. Most places in New England that want a minister, would not be forward to invite one with so chargeable a family, nor one so far advanced in years—being 46 the 5th day of last October. I am fitted for no other business but study, I should make a poor hand at getting a living by any secular employment. We are in the hands of God, and I bless Him, I am not anxious concerning His disposal of us."

During this difficult time Edwards was able to resolve his dismissal in terms of the overruling providence of God. There were *reasons* for what had happened, and his writings reveal his understanding of these reasons. Edwards was misrepresented by those who sought to oust him, and they were a strong, powerful group of persuasive leaders in the Church, some of whom could rightly be called "crafty designing men." Existing prejudices of tradition also served to foster strife and controversy. Edwards understood only too well what was taking place. "Some [of the Church people] were so confused," he wrote, that "without check of conscience, they came to look on their zeal against me as virtue."

Jonathan and Sarah had faced the question whether in severe trials they "could cheerfully resign all to God," and the year 1750 was certainly to bring them to the place where they had to confront this. In his own words, he had received "the largest salary of any country minister in New England," and everything points to the need for that when one considers the care of such a large family; moreover, they received travelers throughout their years in the manse, and this added to their household expenses. Now that income was ended. And many months after his dismissal Edwards was still without any regular means of support.

When a friend wrote asking him to consider moving to Scotland, he replied that moving with his "numerous family, over the Atlantic" would present "many difficulties that I shrink at." He was being realistic.

There were some who urged him to stay in the town and start a second church. This "project" was strongly urged upon him by Colonel Timothy Dwight, who even offered to divide his own salary in order to make this possible. To his credit, Jonathan Edwards at no time even considered this as an option.

121

Five months later, in November 1750, the Edwardses' daughter, Mary, married Timothy Dwight. She was sixteen and the groom—the six-foot, four-inch son of Edwards's friend and neighbor—was twenty-four. This marriage was to leave a deep imprint upon history. Their first son, another Timothy, was to become president of Yale and author of the hymn "I Love Thy Kingdom, Lord," an anthem deeply expressive of the church life in which his mother had grown up.

Of interest is the fact that Mary Edwards Dwight's grandson, Sereno E. Dwight, was to become her father's principal biographer almost eighty years later. In writing about this dismissal from Northampton, Sereno Dwight explains as follows: "The question in controversy, between Mr. Edwards and his people, was one of vital importance to the purity and prosperity of the Christian Church. Wherever the lax method of admission has prevailed, all distinction between the church and the world has soon ceased, and both have been blended together. This question had never been thoroughly examined; and it needed some mind of uncommon power, to exhibit the truth with regard to it, in a light too strong to be ultimately resisted." Jonathan Edwards had that kind of mind albeit he came to his conclusion slowly, reluctantly, empirically, that is, based on experience and his observations as to what had been taking place for far too long.

Edwards's fundamental explanation of what had happened was that God had permitted the weaknesses within the Northampton congregation in order to expose the evil of spiritual pride:

The people have, from the beginning, been well instructed; having had a name, for a long time, for a very knowing people; and many have appeared them, persons of good abilities; and many, born in the town, have been promoted to places of public trust: they have been a people distinguished on this account. These things have been manifestly abused to nourish the pride of their natural temper, which had made them more difficult and unmanageable. . . . In latter times, the people have had more to feed their pride. They have grown a much greater and more wealthy people than formerly, and are become more extensively famous in the world, as a people that have excelled in gifts and grace, and had God extraordinarily among them; which has insensibly engendered and nourished spiritual pride, that grand inlet of the devil in the hearts of men, and avenue of all manner of mischief among a professing people. Spiritual pride is a most monstrous thing. If it be not discerned, and vigorously opposed, in the beginning, it very often soon raises persons above their teachers, and supposed spiritual fathers, and sets them out of the reach of all rule and instruction, as I have seen in innumerable instances. And there is this inconvenience, attending the publishing of narratives of a work of God among a people, (such is the corruption that is in the hearts of men, and even of good men,) and there is great danger of their making

123

*it an occasion of spiritual pride. There is great
reason to think that the Northampton people
have provoked God greatly against them, by
trusting in their privileges and attainments. And
the consequences may well be a warning to all
God's people, far and near, that hear of them.*

This is not to imply that Jonathan Edwards attributed
all the blame for the turn of events and the dismissal to
the people. As he looked back from the vantage point of
greater maturity (writing in 1751), he spoke of his lack
of judgment and discretion in some respects, and that his
own confidence in himself "was a great injury to me; and
in other respects my diffidence of myself injured me."

He spoke of his failure to act on his own judgment,
and that he "had no strength to oppose received notions,
and established customs, and to testify boldly against
some glaring false appearances, and counterfeits of religion, till it was too late. . . . If I had had more experience,
and ripeness of judgment and courage, I should have
guided my people in a better manner, and should have
guarded them better from Satan's devices, and prevented
the spiritual calamity of many souls, and perhaps the
eternal ruin of some of them; and have done what would
have tended to lengthen out the tranquility of the town."

This was very gracious of Jonathan Edwards, but
despite such admissions, it is safe to say that he listened
to the voice of his own conscience, which he felt was
God speaking to him. Through circumstances not of his
making, he had to stand quite alone in the leadership of
the Northampton congregation. When he finally acted

upon the firm conviction that a wrong principle of admission to the Lord's Table imperils the whole nature of the church, and acted upon this—which was a firm biblical conviction—he was ousted.

Patricia J. Tracy has written an especially apt, "final analysis" of Jonathan Edwards's dismissal from Northampton. "The tragedy of Jonathan Edwards," she writes, was that he was so clearly a product of the changing patterns of authority and community life in eighteenth-century New England. He was more like a revolutionary than a Patriarch, but he thought of himself as a Patriarch."

The Edwards family remained in the town of Northampton through the greater part of 1751 and, strange as it may seem, Jonathan was still supplying the Northampton pulpit until mid-November 1750. Twelve of those sermons still survive. In another letter to Erskine, Jonathan Edwards explains, "They have asked me to preach the greater part of the time since my dismission, when I have been at home; but it has seemed to be with much reluctance that they have come to me, and only because they could not get the pulpit supplied otherwise; and they have asked me only from sabbath to sabbath."

While the parish continued to consider candidates to replace him, he was being considered for posts in Canaan, Connecticut, and Lunenburg, Virginia, as well as the position in Scotland. But no calls initially came. The truth was that for all his fame and brilliance, Jonathan Edwards was clearly too controversial for most congregations.

And then the most unusual opportunity of all was offered to him. It seemed so unlike anything suited for the Reverend Mr. Jonathan Edwards.

Stockbridge, the frontier site of a mission to the Housatonic Indians and the home of a few white families, had lacked a missionary for two years. Jonathan Edwards was familiar with what had been taking place since 1737 out in that frontier village located about 160 miles in the wilderness west of Boston, and about sixty miles from Northampton. In fact, Stockbridge had come about as a result of the now-deceased Colonel John Stoddard and his friendly interest in the Indians. Jonathan had attended a meeting in Stoddard's home in 1734, when the need for a mission was presented. The Northampton church had, in fact, taken this work under their wings, as it were, as a mission project.

At Colonel Stoddard's funeral, Jonathan Edwards stated, "He had a far greater knowledge than any other person in the land of the several nations of Indians in these northern parts of America." The Indians also knew John Stoddard better than any other white man. He had a vision of the day when the frontiers would no more need the militia but be secured by the goodwill of the Indians themselves. But he had told Edwards that for such an interracial bond to come about, there needed first to be a unity in the knowledge of God. Stoddard maintained that conversion to Christ would bring blessings to nations as well as to individuals. It was a theme Jonathan Edwards could endorse wholeheartedly.

Stoddard was acting on behalf of the Commissioners for Indian Affairs at Boston, which was a body acting as an agent for the "Society in London for Propagating the Gospel in New England." As a result of that 1734 meeting, which Jonathan Edwards attended, John Sergeant

126

was sent to these Housatonics or "River Indians" to aid in establishing a settlement and a school at a site in the woods between two ranges of the Berkshires. Jonathan was also aware that the Housatonics were few in number in Stockbridge (less than fifty when John Sergeant first reached them in late 1734), but the numbers grew and as Colonel Stoddard had foreseen, there was the potential to reach out to such larger tribes as the Mohawks and the Iroquois. Sergeant had died in 1749 at the age of thirty-eight, and there was no immediate successor. And so, when Samuel Hopkins, Edwards's friend, made the recommendation to the Boston Commissioners, it was a proposal they seriously considered.

Jonathan Edwards did not immediately accept the invitation to undertake this missionary work. However, something had stirred within him, and instead of waiting for spring, he left home amid the snows of January 1751 to review the situation for himself at Stockbridge. Perhaps the Lord was truly calling him to this remote mission outpost.

fourteen

Many thoughts must have rushed through Sarah Edwards's mind as she watched her husband go through the gate of their Northampton home on his way to Stockbridge. To use Miller's comparison, Jonathan was traveling "as deep into America as though in 1851 a man had gone, let us say, from Albany to the Dakotas." It was to be a long, lonely trip, following the Connecticut River trail. Tears no doubt were rolling down Sarah's face. She likely watched until he was almost out of sight, when he turned to wave a final farewell. Then she went back inside to quiet their ten-month-old son, Pierrepont. To her child she may have said, "We can trust the leadings of Providence."

Names might have flashed through her thoughts as she stood there rocking the baby back and forth, his head resting on her shoulder: such dear departed loved ones as Grandfather Stoddard and Uncle John Stoddard; relatives who had made the situation so unthinkably difficult, the Williams clan and Joseph Hawley and his mother, Rebecca; townspeople whose loudly raised voices still rang in her ears, Seth Pomeroy and Timothy Root; dear friends and family members who stood by so lovingly, Colonel Dwight, who was now also her son-in-law, and David Brainerd and dear Jerusha, both with the Lord. The faces of the church family flashed before her, fleeting images both disturbing and comforting. And then she thought of her dear daughter, Sarah, her own namesake, waiting for Jonathan in Stockbridge. . . . Yes, Sarah will be there to greet him, she may have consoled herself, to take his wet coat, to brush off the snow, to hug and welcome him with good food and love. How she missed her eldest daughter since her marriage to Elihu Parsons in June 1750. Now how grateful she was that Elihu and Sarah were established and she was assured her dear husband would receive loving care.

And what was Jonathan Edwards thinking as he bent his head against the January wind and snow, his trusty horse picking her way on the river trail? He'd achieved something of an international reputation, but now he was contemplating becoming a backwoods missionary preacher. Although there was much work to be done, in his heart he knew he'd be leaving behind many opportunities for stimulating intellectual exchange. Not the least of his concerns was the ruggedness of frontier life. Would his dear wife and precious children be equal to it, especially the thought of living among the Indians? Fear was not a word in his vocabulary—unless it was to talk of the "fear of the Lord," but that was a good kind of fear. Still, he did want some reasonable assurance that his wife and children would be safe in this outermost edge of civilized America.

As he reflected on conversations he'd had in the past with Colonel Stoddard, he knew that the missionaries' aim was to bring Christianity and civilization to these Indians. But Edwards also knew that the government expected them to educate the Housatonics and the "Six Nations" Indians, among them the Iroquois and Mohawks, in the ways of peace, which might be worth as much to the situation on the nearby borders as a whole regiment of militia. At the time the French were vying with the English for the allegiance of the Indians. Jonathan's benevolence to the Indians was necessary to persuade them to trust the goodwill of the English.

Jonathan Edwards did not fully know the extent of what this responsibility would entail as he came within sight of the Stockbridge mission. But he was soon to find out.

His tired horse carried him along. Although his beaver hat protected his head and ears, he was nonetheless cold and tired. The mission stood in the center of the town, such as it was. Around it were huddled the wigwams of the Indians who received blankets and food as they needed, but otherwise still lived their tribal life with little modification. As he passed some of them, he nodded pleasantly, but he already knew that they neither spoke nor understood English.

He noted that the village of the whites was entirely separate, "a village within a village, dependent on itself for whatever had justified migration to this lonely spot," as Winslow describes it. Looking up at a hill not too far away, he noted a fine home and concluded correctly that this was where Ephraim Williams lived, the head of the Stockbridge branch of the family. Ephraim had arrived in Stockbridge in 1737 and had initially been allotted 150 acres. Now, contrary to rulings of the government, he already had acquired four hundred acres by purchasing Indian land. His daughter, Abigail, had been married to the now-deceased Reverend John Sergeant, and she also owned a fine home. The other member of the Williams clan was Ephraim, Jr., the town's representative to the General Court.

The family was obviously the most influential in the settlement, as Jonathan was soon to learn. Timothy Woodbridge, a friend of the late David Brainerd's as well as Stockbridge's schoolmaster and deacon, expressed to Jonathan his concerns over the Williams family, who viewed Stockbridge as their private preserve.

Letters from Abigail Sergeant and Ephraim Williams, Jr. to those involved in the securing of a replacement for John Sergeant revealed their sentiments and bias toward Jonathan Edwards before he ever set foot in their midst. Jonathan surely must have felt their initial hostility at the outset on this visit. On the other hand, there is little in the record that reveals the reticence of the Williams clan as he moved among them on that exploratory visit. In fact, Ephraim wrote a letter following that visit in which he states that "since they are so set on him," and because from his viewpoint the settlement of such a well-known figure in their district could prove a business asset in the future, "raising the price of my land," they should consent to his coming. Such motivation was, of course, to be suspect, and Jonathan Edwards was no fool. Even though he didn't know the reasoning behind this tolerant attitude, he would have sensed something amiss.

Abigail Sergeant, in a letter to Ezra Stiles on February 15, 1751, admitted that Jonathan was not the man whom she had anticipated. "Mr. Edwards is now with us. He has conducted [himself] with wisdom and prudence; and, I must confess, I am not a little disappointed in him. He is learned, polite, and free in conversation, and more catholic than I had supposed." Still, even though they showed some evidence of a conciliatory attitude, there was a network of minor hostilities that had crossed and recrossed the family alliances. Jonathan was not without grounds for remaining apprehensive of the influence of the Williams clan.

Casting his eyes about Stockbridge one last time before leaving for Northampton, Jonathan Edwards set out unsettled in his mind. Still confident of divine Providence, he was also surprisingly realistic. He had plenty of time to mull everything over in his head as he and his horse headed back over the river trail he had followed in January. It was now March 1751, and he had reached no conclusion as to his duty.

fifteen

Uncertainty best describes Jonathan Edwards's state of mind upon his return to Northampton. Even so, there was a tug on his heart and he was sensitive to that. Sensing this uncertainty, his son-in-law, Colonel Dwight, and his dear friend, Dr. Mather, renewed their hopes of starting another church in Northampton. Following the protocol of their day, they pressed for another Council to be held to consider the possibility of a second church.

Writing to Joseph Hawley, who had been a leader in gaining his dismissal from the Northampton church, Jonathan penned,

> *I had not refused the invitation to Stock-*
> *bridge, or neglected that opportunity. I had no*
> *inclination or desire to settle. . .at Northampton,*
> *but a very great opposition in my mind to it,*

abundantly manifested in what I continually said to them on occasion of their great and constant urgency.

It was much more agreeable to my inclination to settle at Stockbridge and, though I complied to the calling of a Council to advise in the affair. . .[it was] with a view to these two things: 1. To quiet the minds of those, who in so trying a time had appeared my steadfast friends, that they might not always think exceedingly hardly of me. And 2. The Country having been filled with gross misrepresentations of [the] controversy between me and my people, and the affair of my dismission, and the grounds of it, to the great wounding of my character at a distance, I was willing some ministers of chief note should come from different parts of the country, and be upon the spot, and see the true state of things with their own eyes.

Jonathan and Sarah had faced the question long years before as to whether in severe trials they "could cheerfully resign all to God." Jesus Christ promised, "Blessed are you when men shall persecute you," and what happened in Northampton was unmerited persecution of a sort. Turnbull states that time has vindicated Edwards in his view of the truth and justified his spirit in the midst of controversy. Only now do we see that there is a failure that is blessed of God. Jonathan Edwards was no stiff-necked, autocratic, unbending individual. He had the heart of a humble man who would do what he was called to do and say what he felt God would have him say. He didn't show an arrogant, self-willed spirit that disregarded Providence or human counsel.

More than one writer points out that there was something pathetic in the spectacle of America's premier theologian having to take measures to defend himself against the breath of this scandal. Edwards acted very judiciously. Meanwhile, behind the scene, he was quietly pursuing a move to Stockbridge. He had now had ample time to weigh everything and to wait upon "divine Providence," coming to the conclusion that he was to accept the formal offer. In fact, he had already consulted the Governor of the Province, Sir William Pepperell, on the subject.

Before accepting the offer, he had some legitimate concerns that he wanted to see addressed. He sought assurance from the governor that there was an ongoing commitment to the Indian settlement in what was a comparatively unprotected region. He was also a practical man and he needed some assurance that the Stockbridge church was united, although he had seen little evidence of spiritual purpose among them. There wasn't even a parsonage at Stockbridge to which he could take his family. His property in Northampton hadn't sold and he didn't have the resources to build a home in Stockbridge until that happened.

Notwithstanding these concerns, he felt more and more drawn to Stockbridge, sensing, no doubt, that a ministry there would lead to a fulfillment of his own long-standing prayer (which he had shared with David Brainerd) for the advancement of the Gospel among the Indians. He had a heart for missions.

But he also more than likely looked upon Stockbridge as something of a philosopher's paradise where books could be written. It was to be here in the modest house of a missionary, in a closet seven feet by three and a half feet, in loneliness, and a period of exile of sorts, that he set down the results of almost forty years' study.

The Council with whom he met in Northampton, not surprisingly, advised Jonathan Edwards to accept Stockbridge, which confirmed his own private decision. The date was May 19, 1751. By July, Edwards was already in Stockbridge, leaving his family behind to dispose of their home and property. Unknown to him, right at the time he was making the decision to go to Stockbridge, Presbyterians in Virginia, led by young Samuel Davies, were raising funds for the support of Jonathan and his family. Moreover, in a July 4, 1751, letter from Davies to Joseph Bellamy, Davies reveals his desire to place the leadership of that church in Virginia in Edwards's hands. Davies wrote, "Of all the men I know in America, he appears to me the most fit for this place; and, if he could be obtained on no other condition, I would cheerfully resign him my place, and cast myself into the wide world once more. Fiery, superficial ministers will never do in these parts: they might do good; but they would do much more harm. We need the deep judgment and calm temper of Mr. Edwards among us. . . ."

Murray states that Edwards and Davies would have been a mighty combination in the furtherance of the Gospel in the South, but it was not to be. Jonathan, again writing to his Scottish friend Erskine, explained that he was already installed at Stockbridge before the messenger came with the Virginia invitation.

More encouragement came to Jonathan from friends in Scotland who voiced deep concern. With characteristic Scottish generosity, funds were raised for the Edwards family, leaving Glasgow toward the end of March 1751. Mail traveled slowly, of course, in those days, and on July 13, 1751, Edwards wrote Mr. William Hogg in Edinburgh to express his deep gratitude for this concern and generosity. (Mr. Hogg was a merchant in Castle Hill, much loved by evangelicals.) In his letter, Jonathan Edwards spoke of how this "excit[ed] our admiration [wonder]," and how he and his family regarded this as "the providence of God. . .that God is, as He declares Himself in His Word to be, an all sufficient and faithful God, and that His promise never fails; that we need not fear to trust Him in the way of obedience to Him. . . . In the next place, our gratitude is due to his people, to whom He has given the instruments of His bounty. . .[and] in particular, render thanks to you. . .

"I, with my family, have for this two years past gone through many troubles: But. . .the Lord has not forsaken us, nor suffered us to sink under our trials. He has in many respects exercised a fatherly care of us in our distresses. A door seems to be opened for my further improvement in the work of the ministry in this place which is situated in the north western frontier of New England. . . ."

The letter further proceeds to give an account of the Stockbridge mission and of his hopes "of good things to be accomplished here for the Indians."

Edwards's installation took place on August 8, 1751,

at which time his Stockbridge ministry officially began. He then returned to Northampton and on October 16, the family bade a final farewell. Jonathan Edwards turned his horses out of the King Street yard, with his wife, his small son Pierrepont, and seven other children, and headed toward the wilderness. A chapter was closing on their lives as they shut the doors of the home that had provided so many memories. It was Northampton's most beautiful time of year with the maples turning yellow and scarlet, but it was also the month of October, a month that would always recall for Jonathan Edwards so many memories from the past, including his own birthday, George Whitefield's visit, and David Brainerd's death.

As they rode along, Jonathan told the family more about Stockbridge and the little house he had secured for them where John Sergeant and his wife, Abigail, had lived. He explained that Abigail had moved to a bigger and better house up the hill where her parents and other white families lived. "But we will be on Main Street, near where the Indians live." He was preparing his family for their changed circumstances.

"God settles the bounds of the habitations of His people," he told his family, "and our times are in His hands." He wrote the same thing to his father, still living in East Windsor, adding, "My wife and I are well pleased with our present situation. . . . They like the place far better than they expected. Here, at present, we live in peace; which has of long time been an unusual thing with us."

sixteen

I n Stockbridge Jonathan Edwards faced an insecure future, but he knew with absolute certainty that God was with him. God has His way in the lives of His own, Jonathan believed, and God was surely with the Edwards family.

In July 1751, a month before his installation, in a remarkable show of confidence, Jonathan was appointed by the Boston commissioners to meet with Mohawk chiefs at Albany, in New York province. Following this, he was informed that the commissioners were going to meet with the Indians and him at Stockbridge the week after his installation. In Jonathan's memoirs, there is a scrap of paper that reveals what he wrote and said to the Mohawks, written in his own informal shorthand:

*Your Coming here will rejoyce the Hearts of
all Good men as They will hope it will be a means*

of your coming into greater Light & Knowledge in the Xtian Religion and so be a means of your Et[ernal] *salvation and Happiness.*

We don't desire to keep you from the Kn[owledge] *of the Bible the Word of G. as the French Priests do their Indians. We are willing that you could read the word of G. as well as we & know as much as we.*

While I continue here I shall be willing to come from time to time & to do my utmost to instruct you in the true Xtian Relig[ion].

At the conference one chief asked the commissioners "to promise nothing but what the government would certainly perform." In view of past failures on the part of the English, it was time to show that the chief's request was not needless. But Jonathan Edwards was a man of his word, and the record shows that his first efforts among the Indians were full of promise.

Within three weeks of his installation, he wrote the Boston commissioners, addressing the situation at the mission and proposing a plan that he felt would end the Williamses' domination. The Boston commissioners had general supervision of all matters that were pertinent to the Indian settlements and power to disburse all monies. His suggestions initially were meant to improve internal affairs. Since Sergeant's death, there had been little unity among the workers at the mission and the settlers in the community. His work was surely cut out for him.

The duties of Jonathan Edwards in Stockbridge presented unique challenges. He was responsible to the

Society for the Propagation of the Gospel in London, as well as Boston, and communication with these remote centers of authority meant long delays. A situation could change completely before a reply came. The Boston commissioners were in sympathy with the work of Jonathan Edwards and those assisting him, but in reality they were more interested in Indian trade and Indian loyalty. To them, the mission was a valuable means to achieve their ends; to Jonathan Edwards, "God's work" was not just a profitable investment.

One of his recommendations was that Major Joseph Dwight, a man competent for the post of resident agent for the commissioners, be appointed right away. Major Dwight arrived, full of enthusiasm at the opportunity to sit under the ministry of Edwards for whom he had long professed a high regard. Jonathan hoped this appointment would bring about some impartial and profitable control. He also hoped this would increase his chances for some personal peace.

What Jonathan Edwards could not foresee was that the high-spirited widow Abigail Williams Sergeant would cast an approving and inviting eye at the major and that he would fall under her charms and marry her. Almost immediately the Williams family had an ally in their new son-in-law, and Jonathan, the missionary, had another opponent. It was an untenable position. Would the Boston Commissioners for Indian Affairs pay attention to him, or would they put more stock in Major Dwight, the resident agent? Of greater concern was what would become of his promises to the Indians, plans that were intended to educate the Indian children and improve relations with the Indians, while instructing them in the Bible.

Meanwhile Jonathan Edwards made plans for a suitable home to be built for his large family on a tract of land near the center of the town, and work was begun. When it was finished, he petitioned the General Court that the home be purchased for a parsonage, but the petition was denied. It came as a shock. He put his finger on the problem and wrote to friends. Colonel Ephraim Williams was present at the session where his proposal was discussed, and Jonathan explained that Williams was "constantly busy with the Representatives, with his Lime-juice Punch & Wine. Objections were made against the Petition which could come from none but He." It was a heartbreaking defeat. Such a measure only contributed to Jonathan's financial problems, difficulties exacerbated by his considerably reduced salary.

The English-speaking people, and notably the Williams clan, mostly lived above the straggly little town, on Prospect Hill. Edwards began referring to them as "the people on the hill," a euphemism that fit, for it was a stately residence, a virtual fort, which dominated the valley. He already knew that the Indians' misgivings were true: The mission was, for all intents and purposes, only another stage in white expansion. Ephraim Williams had never enjoyed the trust that the Indians showed toward Timothy Woodbridge, the schoolteacher. By the time the Edwards family arrived, there was an open rupture between Timothy Woodbridge and Ephraim Williams. Woodbridge rightly regarded Williams's attitude towards the Indians as a threat to the mission. Another problem that asserted itself came as a surprise. Elisha Williams, nephew of the strong-willed Ephraim Williams, Sr., had been in London during the years 1749–50 where he had been treated as a celebrity. He was appointed to the board of the Society for the Propagation of the Gospel in New England and, unknown to Edwards, was to be one of his overseers. At Elisha Williams's recommendation, his uncle, Ephraim Williams, was appointed as well.

The potential for strife was growing. Elisha also recommended to the London board that a female school should be started in Stockbridge with yet another Williams at its head. It was to be none other than Abigail Sergeant Dwight! Moreover, they had sealed the arrangement by paying her a year's salary in advance "for her trouble."

There was also a Mohawk boarding school in the town managed by a Captain Martin Kellogg (another confidant and relative by marriage of Ephraim Williams). It didn't take Edwards long to discover the incompetence and illiteracy of Kellogg, and this he reported to the Boston commissioners early on. They sent the young and able Gideon Hawley to take over, but when Hawley arrived, Kellogg objected and insisted that he was still the superintendent, answerable to a man by the name of Hollis, who lived 3,000 miles away in England! Hollis was a Baptist minister of some means who funded the Mohawk boarding school as a mission project.

On February 18, 1752, Edwards wrote to the Boston commissioners, and six days later he also wrote Joseph Paine, an official for the London Society. The latter letter was a masterpiece in summarizing the conflict between

145

commercial and religious interests, the waste of public money, and the duplication of effort by rival missionaries. Much as he needed and wanted to devote himself to the pastoral duties of the mission, he saw very clearly the problems in which he found himself embroiled, all unwittingly.

As he wrote his letters, he not only had a grasp of the larger aspects of the missionary problems, he also had the detachment of a good administrator. Jonathan had shown himself fully capable of handling the minutiae of practical affairs facing conditions as they were and acting very responsibly.

By the time he had been at Stockbridge two years, Edwards concluded [that] events were fast shaping "to establish a Dominion of the Family of Williams over Stockbridge affairs." Ephraim Williams and Joseph Dwight were grafters and land-grabbers, to use the descriptive terminology of Miller. They maintained a despotic control of both the town and the mission, a stranglehold that was highly profitable to themselves but fatal to the peace of the town and the success of the mission.

Edwards had a legitimate concern for the Indians. The Mohawks had been lured into the settlement to spare the frontier more massacres like those that had occurred fifty years earlier at Deerfield. When Jonathan pressed the issue about the deep distrust that the Indians had with regard to Ephraim Williams and Joseph Dwight, the commissioners began to listen to his charges. Moreover, in the spring of 1753, the boys' boarding school was destroyed by fire, and it appeared that violence was near at hand. As a result of all this, the commissioners looked at the array of facts before them, their eyes were opened, and the Williams clan was powerless. As Winslow explains, "Their domination was swiftly ended."

Even with all of this going on, somehow Jonathan Edwards managed to find time to write. He accomplished his final work on the communion controversy entitled *Misrepresentations Corrected, and Truth Vindicated.*

He continued to be an avid reader. Edwards was a lover of books, but the aim of the hours he spent in reading and studying was for spiritual enlargement. He valued his library as a man enjoys and values his friends. He was greatly dependent upon his friends across the ocean to send him books since the "old world" still had a monopoly on printing and distribution. He wanted to be kept informed, and he was. As a zestful enthusiast of books, he catalogued what he read, and in a reference in his will, his books were valued at eighty pounds sterling, consisting of an estimate of 336 volumes and 536 pamphlets. (Considering, however, that this will was written some years before his death, this cannot be considered entirely accurate and up to date.)

Samuel Hopkins, the longtime friend of Edwards, has written: "He read all the books, especially books of divinity, that he could procure, from which he might hope to derive any aid in his pursuit of knowledge. . . . Thus he was all his days, like the busy bee, collecting from every opening flower, and storing up a stock of knowledge which was indeed sweet to him, as the honey and the honeycomb. And as he advanced in years and in knowledge, his pen was more and more employed, and his manuscripts grew much faster on his hands." Turnbull points out that the pastoral preacher came to an enlarged ministry through his passion for books and the studious habits that were fed from his library.

In the summer of 1752 Edwards's third daughter, Esther, was married to the thirty-six-year-old Presbyterian minister of Newark and president of the New Jersey College, Aaron Burr. Jonathan was not at the wedding (although his wife was) as he had already promised to be in New York (150 miles from Stockbridge) in September for a meeting with the correspondents of the Society for Propagating Christian Knowledge. He wouldn't have been able to make the journey twice. So when September came, he stayed with the newlyweds in Newark and shared in a meeting of the college trustees at the time of the commencement and at the Presbyterian Synod of New York where he preached.

When he returned to Stockbridge in October, it was to commence with a time of greater family sickness than they had ever known before. His wife was so desperately ill that for a while it seemed her death was imminent. Soon Sarah Parsons, his married daughter, became very sick and his youngest daughter, little Betty, weak since birth, "was brought nigh unto death."

Despite these personal travails, his three years' residence at Stockbridge had earned for Jonathan the confidence and esteem of the congregations among the Indians and the English settlers. He still couldn't speak their language well enough to deliver sermons from the pulpit, but for practical purposes he negotiated in the Housatonic language, and a little in Mohawk, but he always worked with an interpreter. It was a handicap, but the Indians liked him. He was patient and kind. Of interest is that his children all spoke the Indian languages fluently.

Contained in the notes from one of his sermons to the Indians— speaking on 2 Timothy 3:16— is the following:

> *'Tis worth the while to take a great deal of pains to learn to read and understand the Scriptures. I would have all of you think of this. When there is such a book that you may have, how can you be contented without being able to read it?*
>
> *How does it make you feel when you think there is a Book that is God's own Word? . . .*
>
> *Parents should take care that their children learn. . . .*
>
> *This will be the way to be kept from the Devil. . . . Devil can't bear [the Bible.] Kept from Hell. To be happy forever.*
>
> *But if you let the Word of God alone, and never use, and you can't expect the benefits of it. You must not only hear and read, etc., but you must have it sunk down into your heart. Believe. Be affected. Love the Word of God. Written in your heart.*
>
> *Must not only read and hear, but DO the things. Otherwise no good; but will be the worse for it.*
>
> *And you should endeavour to understand. To that end to learn the English tongue. If you had*

*the Bible in your own language, I should not say
so much.*

*Consider how much it is worth the while to
go often to your Bible to hear the great God
Himself speak to you. There you may hear God
speak. How much better must we think this is
than the word of men. Better than the word of
the wisest man of the world.*

How much wiser is God than man.

Here all is true; nothing false.

Here all is wise; nothing foolish.

With the outbreak of the French and Indian War in
1754, the entire mission situation changed abruptly.
Much of the mission work was at a standstill as many of
the Christian Indians enlisted, leaving only a remnant at
Stockbridge. Colonel Ephraim Williams, Sr., in poor
health, had moved to Deerfield. The younger Ephraim
was killed in battle. And Abigail Sergeant Dwight, who
was no heroine, according to Miller, fled the frontier.

The whole New England frontier was in a state of
alarm, and Stockbridge, situated at the outermost reaches,
was considered easy prey.

seventeen

The reality of the war hit close to home in Stockbridge one Sunday morning in September 1754, when some Indians from Canada, doubtless sent by the French, broke in upon the worshippers, between meetings, and fell upon an English family, killing three of them. An hour later these same Indians killed another man. Writing in a letter, Jonathan reported, "We are divided into a great many distinct governments, independent one of another, and, in some respects, of clashing interests. . .[making us] an easy prey to our vigilant, secret, subtle, swift and active, though comparatively small, enemy."

Just when Edwards's leadership was at last bringing everything under control, the French-British relationships exploded into war. The French moved south from Canada and established forts from north to south in the interior for a thousand miles or more. And, just as the British feared,

French influence and control among many Indian tribes proved significant. Another major problem, as Edwards pointed out, was the lack of coordination among the two million English living in the thirteen colonies.

Contributing to the troubled milieu at Stockbridge, at the time of the war's outbreak, Jonathan was suffering from ill health. In his letters can be found these words: "I am still so weak that I can write but with a trembling hand, as you may easily perceive." He referred to his problem as "fits of ague [that] exceedingly wasted my flesh and strength, so that I became like a skeleton." It is felt that this was probably malaria, with intermittent high fevers and shivering. Following the incident at the church on that Sabbath, soldiers had been rushed to Stockbridge and a fort was built around the Edwards home as a place of retreat for others in the event of further attacks. This brought a new set of problems to the already financially plagued Edwards family. The needs of the troops had to be met, including lodging.

In a report to the General Court, Jonathan estimated that no less than eight hundred meals had been served, and the equivalent of twenty-four hours' pasturage for 150 horses provided. While the fort itself was being built, the laborers had consumed 180 more meals, and when building materials ran short, Edwards himself supplied fifteen rods of new log fence, which had cost him ten shillings per rod.

In 1756, during this time of hostilities, Esther Burr, Jonathan and Sarah's newly married daughter, came to Stockbridge to visit. She brought with her her infant son Aaron, who was much later to be the center of so many storms in American history. This would be her first and last visit—she hadn't lived with the Indian danger before, as her sisters had—and she often was beside herself with terror. Like Abigail Dwight, she would have preferred to flee the frontier, but she was an Edwards. Spirited and witty, Esther wrote, "If the Indians get me, they get me, that is all I can say. I am not willing to be butchered by a barbarous enemy nor can't make myself willing!"

Although Stockbridge was to be miraculously preserved, Jonathan still followed political and military events with close attention. More than the personal safety of his family was involved in his watchfulness. Edwards truly had a heart for missions and the North American Indians and for the glory of God in the American nation of the future. If the French were successful, the Indians would be beyond the reach of Gospel preaching and the future for the English-speaking colonies and for Protestantism would be greatly darkened.

As he wrote to his Scottish friend, John Erskine, in April 1755, "The business of the Indian Mission, since I have been here, has been attended with strange embarrassments, such as I never could have expected, or so much as once dreamed of: of such a nature, and coming from such a quarter, that I take no delight in being very particular and explicit about it."

The danger of the powerful Six Nations tribes going over to the French was uppermost in his mind: ". . .which there is the greatest reason to expect, unless the English should exert themselves, vigorously and successfully, against the French in America this year. They seem to be waiting to see whether this will be so or no, in order to determine whether they will entirely desert the English and cleave to the French. And if the Six Nations should forsake the English, it may be expected that the Stockbridge Indians, and almost all the nations of Indians in North America, will follow them. It seems to be the most critical season with the British dominions in America that ever was seen, since the first settlement of these colonies; and all, probably, will depend on the warlike transactions of the present year. What will be done I cannot tell. We are all in commotion, from one end of British America to the other."

During all these years in Stockbridge, the Edwards home was still the haven of hospitality to visitors on horseback, just as it had been in Northampton. Journals and letters from theologians and others of that era reveal that life was pleasant in the family home, and even though the wilderness had its share of inconveniences and problems, Sarah and Jonathan practiced hospitality in the true biblical sense. When the warring factions brought increased danger to this frontier mission outpost, the arrival of visitors was less likely to occur, but Samuel Hopkins and Joseph Bellamy were two such distinguished visitors who came and went a few times in 1755 and 1756. The three men were great friends and always their conversations turned to the writings Jonathan still pursued (as revealed in diaries of Hopkins).

Jonathan continued to work hard to adapt and simplify sermons for the Indians, and the work was bearing fruit. In one letter to Erskine, he noted, "Some of the Stockbridge Indians have of late been under considerable awakenings—two or three elderly men that used to be vicious persons."

The children in Stockbridge, both white and Indian, had classes on the Westminster *Shorter Catechism,* and Jonathan also spent time teaching them writing and spelling. Jonathan Edwards, Jr., was six when the family moved to Stockbridge, and many years later he wrote of his memories of this period: "Stockbridge. . .was inhabited by Indians almost solely, as there were in the town but twelve families of whites, or Anglo Americans, and perhaps one hundred and fifty families of Indians. The Indians being the nearest neighbours, I constantly associated with them; their boys were my daily schoolmates and play-fellows. . . ."

Murray explains, "The value which Edwards placed upon work among the Indians is illustrated by his hopes that Jonathan, Jr. might also be a missionary among them." Edwards's friend Gideon Hawley was making plans to set off deep into the territory of the Delaware Indians, some two hundred miles away, at Onohoquaha on the Susquehanna River. Amazingly, Jonathan and Sarah Edwards had enough confidence in the venturesome Hawley to send nine-year-old Jonathan with him so he could learn the Mohawk language.

A letter from father to son, dated May 27, 1755, has survived, and it shows not only the elder Edwards's fatherly concern, but his spirituality:

Though you are a great way off from us, yet you are not out of our minds: I am full of concern for you, often think of you, and often pray for you. Though you are at so great a distance from us, and from all your relations, yet this is a

155

comfort to us, that the same God that is here is also at Onohoquaha and that though you are out of our sight, and out of our reach, you are always in God's hands, who is infinitely gracious; and we can go to Him, and commit you to His care and mercy. Take heed that you don't forget or neglect Him. Always set God before your eyes, and live in His fear, and seek Him every day with all diligence: for He, and He only can make you happy or miserable, as He pleases; and your Life and Health, and the eternal salvation of your soul and your all in this life and that which is to come depends on His will and pleasure.

Father, mother, and son were reunited in Stockbridge early in 1756.

It is plain to see that Jonathan was always concerned with the spiritual welfare of others. Such love and concern motivated him to look after not only the spiritual needs of the Indians, but also their physical and temporal needs. Thus it was that when the war and the scattering of the Mohawks interfered with educational efforts at Stockbridge, Jonathan Edwards did everything he could to send as many of the Indian boys as possible to his friend Bellamy at a place called Bethlehem.

In a letter accompanying these boys he speaks of their need to learn and continues: "I would also propose the following things, viz. That pains be taken with them to teach them the English tongue, to learn them the meaning of English words and what the name of everything is in English. . .and that they be taught to pray, that you write out for them various forms of prayer, and make them understand them, and turn them after into Indian. And to teach them the. . .Catechism and endeavour as far as may be to make them to understand it. O ask them questions of the scripture history, not only the lessons they read, but the main things in the general history of the Bible in their order."

Edwards had the best interests of these Indian boys at heart. He had the compassion of a father toward them. In all of this he was motivated by Christian love.

In a letter from the period, Edwards expounded on how children should be taught. Children's lessons, he said, must "be rendered pleasant, entertaining and profitable, not a dull, wearisome task, without any suitable pleasure or benefit." He explained that teachers must create an appetite for knowledge, that they must not allow the children to memorize without understanding, nor must they remain aloof from the class by adopting a superior manner. Familiar questions should be put to the child about the subjects of the lesson; and the child should be encouraged, and drawn on, to speak freely, and in his turn also [be allowed] to ask questions for the resolution of his own doubts.

Enough is known from the records of the Stockbridge Indians in later years to provide evidence that Jonathan Edwards's work among them was not in vain. At the end of the century Timothy Dwight was able to write: "Their reverence for him was very great and his family are still regarded by their [Stockbridge] descendants with peculiar respect."

Content to continue his frontier exile, Jonathan had no idea that soon he would be leaving Stockbridge. He had spent seven years among the Indians, years of intense labor on their behalf but also years that resulted in some of his finest writings, including *Freedom of the Will,* the work on which his fame would rest securely for more than a hundred years. One of the last pieces of writing from the Stockbridge era was *God's Last End in Creation,* which Winslow describes as "more alive than any other hundred [pages]." By May 1757 Edwards had finished what would be his last work, *The Great Christian Doctrine of Original Sin Defended.*

His years in Stockbridge had been fraught with conflict, both internal and external, but at the same time God had granted him a place to gather himself together again. Now God was leading Jonathan Edwards to his final destination, a locale far removed from the treacherous frontier.

eighteen

When Esther Edwards married Aaron Burr in 1752, she presented Jonathan with a son-in-law of whom he was very proud. Letters between the two men attest to this bond and their mutual concern for the spiritual welfare of those entrusted to their pastoral care.

Aaron Burr was president of New Jersey College (later to be called Princeton) located in Newark, and he also was pastor of a large Presbyterian church there. Life in that parsonage was cheerful. Like her mother, Esther was a wonderful hostess who showed much discernment on spiritual issues as well.

Esther was very happy to have her father in their home in September 1752. During his stay, Jonathan accompanied Aaron Burr to Philadelphia for a synod meeting, an excursion that resulted in both men returning home ill. Jonathan, who amazingly recovered faster than his son-in-law, managed to preach two sermons from Burr's pulpit while Aaron continued to recuperate.

In October 1755, the Burrs made a visit to Princeton, the future site of New Jersey College, to view the progress of Nassau Hall, as it was to be called. A letter from her parents in Stockbridge urged Esther to come and visit them before the winter of 1756, when she would be moving to Princeton. It wasn't until November 1756 that the college was moved and Aaron and Esther Burr with their two children were settled. Their lives were busy, as Aaron Burr also cared for a congregation two-thirds the size of his church in Newark, and he had seventy students in the college.

On February 8, 1757, a revival began in the college that Aaron Burr likened to the Great Awakening. Jonathan received news of this revival from both his daughter and son-in-law in separate letters with much interest. Each knew the eagerness there would be in Stockbridge to receive this news. Burr, mindful of what he had learned from his father-in-law about revivals, was cautious about any forms of "wild-fire" or announcements of numbers converted. He wrote, "Much old experience has taught me to judge of these things more by the fruits than any account of experience for a short season. . . ."

Jonathan, far from distrusting the reports from Aaron and Esther, wrote about this to John Erskine: "Amidst the great darkness which attends the state of things in British America, God is causing some light to arise." Even before the awakening at Princeton College, Edwards had recorded in one of his notebooks that "the erecting of N. Jersey College" was a hopeful sign of the spread of the

Gospel into the American world in preparation for the "glorious days" of the Church. His response to this revival news at the college clearly showed his faith in the possibility and in the necessity of true revivals. He was overjoyed when his son-in-law was able to come and visit him in Stockbridge in late summer 1757 and provide firsthand news about the awakening at the college.

The weather was very hot and sultry, and perhaps owing to such conditions, less than a month after his Stockbridge visit, on September 24, 1757, Aaron Burr was dead at the age of forty-one. Esther Burr was now a twenty-five-year-old widow; her small daughter and son were fatherless. Greatly bereaved, she wrote the shocking news to her parents: "God has seemed sensibly near in such a supporting and comforting manner that I think I have never experienced the like."

Four days after Burr's death, the first commencement of the college at Princeton took place. The trustees lost no time in choosing a successor: Seventeen of the twenty trustees present voted to send a letter of invitation to Jonathan Edwards.

A great supporter of the college from its inception, Jonathan had been mentioned for the post in 1748, before Aaron Burr was elected. Even though Stockbridge was 150 miles from Newark, he remained in close touch with and always preached at the college on his visits to that part of the country, including several commencement ceremonies. Certainly, Jonathan was the most prominent candidate considered for the position. His theological views and evangelistic emphasis in preaching presented no problems to the trustees.

While he must have felt honored and pleased, he was, however, deeply troubled as evidenced by the long letter he wrote dated October 19, 1757, sent immediately in response. Biographers consider his reply a masterpiece in self-analysis and a statement of the plan he had in his heart and mind for the books he wanted to write in the remaining years of his life, however long or short that might be.

Jonathan wasted no effort in trying to disqualify himself. Candidly explaining his personal circumstances, he wrote, "We have scarcely got over the trouble and damages sustained by our removal from Northampton, and have but just begun to have our affairs in a comfortable situation for a subsistence in this place. . . ."

He then set forth in detail what he honestly felt were his "defects," as he called them. He called attention to his constitution and the weaknesses of which "my own heart is conscious," among them sluggishness and low spirits at times, that "unfitted" him for conversation "and particularly for the government of a college." He felt he lacked the alertness that such responsibilities demanded. "This makes me shrink at the thoughts of taking upon me, in the decline of life, such a new and great business, attended with such a multiplicity of cares. . . ."

Yet there was another reason why he struggled with this decision and he was equally honest, albeit wordy, about that. To preface his remarks, he explained his method of study by writing, specifically, the way he applied himself "to improve every important hint; pursuing the clue to my utmost, when anything in reading, meditation or conversation, has been suggested to my mind, that seemed to promise light, in any weighty point.—Thus penning what appeared to me my best thoughts, on innumerable subjects for my own benefit. . . ."

His studies, he explained, "have long engaged and swallowed up my mind, and been the chief entertainment and delight of my life." Jonathan then went on to outline three projects dear to his heart: One, an answer to the "prevailing errors of the present day"; two, finishing a work that he had long ago begun, "which I call a *History of the Work of Redemption*"; and three, "the *Harmony of the Old and New Testaments* in three parts."

"My heart is so much in these studies, that I cannot feel willing to put myself into an incapacity to pursue them any more in the future part of my life, to such a degree as I must, if I undertake to go through the same course of employ, in the office of a president, as Mr. Burr did. . . ."

He did propose a plan, however, whereby if he should accept their invitation, he could undertake a general supervision of the college and some limited instruction of classes. Jonathan was well aware of the many teaching and administrative duties that had consumed his son-in-law and perhaps hastened his demise. Aaron Burr had taught every subject to one class at Princeton, besides offering instruction in all languages to the entire college. Jonathan's plan was that he would "merely" instruct the senior class in arts and sciences, take on "the whole work of professor of divinity," and teach Hebrew to the entire college! In the meantime he determined to ask the advice of a number of men whose counsel he greatly valued.

The trustees sent two representatives to present their side in case the Stockbridge church refused to grant a release. A meeting was called at Stockbridge on January 4, 1758, at which time Jonathan again presented what he had already written in the letter to the trustees. The trustees need not have worried: The Stockbridge church felt, without reservation, that it was Jonathan's duty to accept the invitation to the presidency of the college.

Greatly moved by their recommendation, and quite unlike his usual demeanor in the presence of others, Jonathan "fell into tears on the occasion." Four days later, on January 8, 1758, Jonathan Edwards preached his farewell sermon to the Stockbridge church and to the Indians. Recalling this farewell, seventeen-year-old Susannah Edwards wrote: "My father took leave of all his people and family as affectionately as if he knew he should not come again. On the Sabbath afternoon he preached from these words: 'We have no continuing city, therefore let us seek one to come.' The chapter that he read was Acts the 20th. O, how proper: what could he have done more? When he had got out of doors he turned about,—'I commit you to God,' said he."

Within a few days, he was on his way to Princeton in consideration of the urgency of the needs at the college. It was not a good time of year to be traveling on horse-back, but he had traveled before in such weather. It was definitely not a good time to move his entire family, and so he took his departure alone, assuring them that he would send for them hopefully in the spring. There was much for his wife to attend to in his absence, including disposal of the family homestead.

His twenty-one-year-old daughter, Lucy, was already with her widowed sister, Esther Burr, at Princeton. His forty-eight-year-old wife, nineteen-year-old Timothy (who had been ill), seventeen-year-old Susannah, fourteen-year-old Eunice, twelve-year-old Jonathan, eleven-year-old Betty, and his youngest child, eight-year-old Pierrepont remained behind in Stockbridge. His eldest married daughter, thirty-year-old Sarah Parsons, was still living in Stockbridge and could therefore assist her mother. Twenty-four-year-old Mary, who had married Colonel Dwight, still lived in Northampton.

Seven years earlier, as he departed from Northampton, Jonathan had been uncertain of the future for himself and his family, but God had proven faithful. Now he knew what to expect, more or less. The presidency of Princeton awaited him. Honor long overdue America's foremost theologian had come.

But such laudatory treatment was to be shortlived. On February 16, Jonathan Edwards arrived at Princeton, where he was warmly welcomed by Esther and his two grandchildren and by daughter Lucy. The college wasted no time in inducting him into his office in the president's chair. Corporate trustees, friends, and well-wishers of the college were on hand to express their joy at having him in their midst. That week he preached in the college hall and was warmly received by the students. He gave out some questions in divinity to the senior class for which they had to prepare answers to be discussed later, a procedure that met with an enthusiastic response. On Sunday he preached from Hebrews 13:8, "Jesus Christ,

165

the same yesterday, and to day, and for ever." When he concluded his sermon, it was reported that his hearers were surprised to discover that two hours had passed so quickly.

Here he was, back in the civilized world again, in the presence of thinkers and theologians with whom he had always felt the most comfortable. There was sympathy and approval of his views; these were people who had read and studied his writings. It must have been very heartwarming to Jonathan, and the reception signaled a very promising and hopeful beginning.

Yet there was a threat looming on the horizon, a scourge far removed from matters of spirituality. Smallpox was common in the vicinity of Princeton and many people had died from the dreaded disease months earlier during an epidemic. Where there had been no hope of combating this often fatal illness only ten years earlier, a form of inoculation was now available that had met with a good deal of success. But such a procedure was not without risk. Jonathan, ever interested in the progress of medical science, discussed the option of inoculation with his two daughters. At the same time he held legitimate concerns since daughter Lucy had contracted smallpox the preceding summer. A decision was reached and the inoculation performed on February 23, 1758.

The vaccine took successfully, and his daughter Esther was also vaccinated at the same time. It was thought all danger was over until Jonathan came down with a secondary fever. The medical record states "by reason of a number of pustules in his [Jonathan Edwards's] throat, the obstruction was such, that the medicines necessary to

166

check the fever could not be administered."

When he was told that there was no hope of recovery, Jonathan was "a little perplexed for awhile," but his questionings were brief and he characteristically accepted the verdict as the will of God. After enduring a month of painful illness, he called his daughter Lucy to him and she proceeded to soothe his fevered brow, bending over him to hear his words. His throat was so swollen he couldn't even drink sufficiently to stem the fever, yet be able to speak. But he was able to put pen to paper:

Dear Lucy, it seems to me to be the will of God, that I must shortly leave you; therefore give my kindest love to my dear wife, and tell her, that the uncommon union, which has so long subsisted between us, has been of such a nature, as I trust is spiritual, and therefore will continue forever. And I hope she will be supported under so great a trial and submit cheerfully to the will of God.

And as to my children, you are now like to be left fatherless, which I hope will be an inducement to you all, to seek a Father who will never fail you.

And as to my funeral, I would have it to be like Mr. Burr's, and any additional sum of money, that might be expected to be laid out that way, I would have it disposed of to charitable uses.

After giving these messages, Jonathan looked about and said, "Now where is Jesus of Nazareth, my true and never-failing Friend?"

Those at his bedside, believing him to be unconscious, immediately expressed their grief. But Jonathan Edwards would have the final word. "Trust in God," he said, "and you need not fear."

epilogue

Jonathan Edwards passed from life to death and into heaven to be with his Lord forevermore on March 22, 1758. He was fifty-four years old. That same day, the attending physician, Dr. William Shippen from Princeton, wrote to the newly widowed Sarah Edwards:

This afternoon, between two and three o'clock, it pleased God to let him sleep in that dear Lord Jesus, whose kingdom and interest he has been faithfully and painfully serving all his life. And never did any mortal man more fully and clearly evidence the sincerity of all his professions, by one continued, universal, calm, cheerful resignation and patient submission to the Divine will, through each stage of his disease, than he. . . . Death has certainly lost its sting, as to him.

The mail being what it was, it wasn't until April 3 that Sarah received the heartbreaking news. She then penned letters to her daughters in Princeton and to Mary in Northampton (and doubtless also intended for all her children), comforting them with these words:

What shall I say? A holy and good God has covered us with a dark cloud. O that we may kiss the rod, and lay our hands on our mouths! The Lord has done it. He has made me adore His goodness, that we had him so long. But my God lives; and He has my heart. O what a legacy my husband, and your father, has left us! We are all given to God; and there I am, and love to be.

One daughter would never receive her mother's letter. Sixteen days after her father's death, Esther was gone also, dying from an unknown cause. Her death, which was not the result of her smallpox inoculation, was so completely unexpected that it was an even greater shock to her family than the loss of Jonathan Edwards. Esther's two children, Sally, aged four, and Aaron, two (who would become the vice-president of the United States), were taken to Philadelphia, but there is no record showing to whom they were delivered. Jonathan Edwards was buried at Princeton near the graves of Aaron and Esther Burr.

Still more sorrow was to come to the family of Jonathan Edwards. That summer, following the deaths of her husband and daughter, Sarah Edwards journeyed to Princeton. Possibly Lucy was still there to meet her

170

mother, and the college trustees would have seen to her welfare as well. After viewing the graves of her loved ones, Sarah went to Philadelphia, presumably to collect her two orphaned grandchildren. A letter from Sarah Parsons written to her sister, Mary Dwight, reveals what happened next: "Although in good health when she began the journey, she became violently ill with dysentery upon her arrival in Philadelphia, and died on October 2nd. . . ."

Her body was taken to Princeton and buried beside the graves of her husband, her daughter, and her son-in-law. As Samuel Hopkins, Edwards's much-loved friend, wrote, "Surely America is greatly emptied by these deaths."

It is said that in terms of his own family heritage, Jonathan Edwards should have had a longer life span. His father died two months before him, at eighty-nine; his mother lived to be ninety-eight. Grandfather Solomon Stoddard had been eighty-five; Grandmother Warham-Stoddard, ninety-two. Five of his sisters and four of his children lived past their seventies. Yet he was dead at fifty-four.

Of Jonathan and Sarah's children, Betty died at the age of fourteen while living in Northampton at the home of her sister Mary. Mary Dwight died at Northampton in 1807, five years after a glorious revival at Yale, where her son Timothy was president. Sarah Parsons of Stockbridge later moved to Goshen, Massachusetts, where she lived until her death in 1805. Lucy Edwards returned to Stockbridge, married a Woodbridge, bore nine children, and died in 1786. Of the seven daughters,

Eunice lived the longest, dying in North Carolina in 1822, at the age of seventy-nine. The three Edwards sons, Timothy, Jonathan, and Pierrepont, rose to prominence in public life, and Jonathan succeeded his father in Christian ministry.

According to Turnbull, a study of Edwards's descendants is a testimony to the godly and intellectual influence of his life and character: "There are among them presidents of eight colleges, about one hundred college professors, more than one hundred lawyers, sixty physicians, thirty judges, eighty holders of important public office, twenty-five officers in the army and navy, and almost innumerable clergymen and missionaries." Turnbull's source for such data came from a 1903 article by E. A. Winship in the magazine *World's Work*. One can only imagine what has transpired since then!

Despite the longevity of his predecessors, Jonathan undoubtedly entertained the possibility of an early demise. Aware of what he called "the Infirmity of his Constitution," five years before his death he had put his affairs in order by the writing of his will. The inventory of his personal effects speaks eloquently of the simplicity with which he conducted his life. He was not a man of the world; he was always concerned with the inner man and his relationship to God. The list reads like this:

"Best Beever Hat" and "One D[itto] poorer"
"Best Wigg" and "One D[itto] poorer"
"Great Coat" and "Old D[itto]"
"Black Coat" and "Two poorer D[itto]"
"1 pr. Specticles" and "pr D[itto]"

He had a pocket compass, but no watch; two pairs of knee buckles, but no other jewelry. His wealth, if it could be called such, was in his published books, published sermon booklets, and unpublished manuscripts. He left a legacy for college or for an apprenticeship to law or medicine, and if any one of his three sons should "take up Learning," the entire library should be his. This share fell to his second son and namesake, Jonathan. (This son's own life closely paralleled his father's, even to dismissal after a twenty-six-year pastorate and death soon after election to a college presidency.)

Of his writings, it fell to Samuel Hopkins, supported by another great friend, Joseph Bellamy, to take the lead in having more of Edwards's writings published.

Turnbull has summarized magnificently what the life of Jonathan Edwards was all about:

> *An example of one who lived by the highest standards of the ministry; a disciplined and dedicated pastor; an intelligent and passionate preacher of the Gospel; a pastor who believed profoundly that the sermon was an agency of God in the conversion of souls; an evangelical mystic, a man who knew experimentally the work of God's Spirit in the soul; and a man who proclaimed the whole counsel of God, not shunning the difficult and unpopular themes of revelation.*

In short, Jonathan Edwards preached what he keenly felt, believing that he was a voice for God. And what a voice he was.

appendix A

Jonathan Edwards's *Resolutions* (referred to in various places throughout this book) ran from 1722 to 1735 (with only six entries after 1725). Probably it began at an earlier date, but nothing survived apart from what Sereno Dwight, Edwards's great-grandson, printed. The original diary, which Dwight had, is now lost.

The following extracts may be taken as representative of the spirit of the whole. The ardency of commitment and desire is plainly evident.

> *Being sensible that I am unable to do anything without God's help, I do humbly entreat Him, by His grace, to enable me to keep these Resolutions, so far as they are agreeable to His will, for Christ's sake. . . .*
>
> *Resolved, Never to do any manner of thing, whether in soul or body, less or more, but what*

tends to the glory of God, nor be, nor suffer it, if I can possibly avoid it.

Resolved, Never to lose one moment of time, but to improve it in the most profitable way I possibly can.

Resolved, To live with all my might, while I do live.

Resolved, To strive every week to be brought higher in religion, and to a higher exercise of grace, than I was the week before.

Resolved, Never to say anything at all against any body, but when it is perfectly agreeable to the highest degree of Christian honour, and of love to mankind, agreeable to the lowest humility, and sense of my own faults and failings, and agreeable to the golden rule.

Resolved, To inquire every night, as I am going to bed, wherein I have been negligent— what sin I have committed—and wherein I have denied myself; also, at the end of every week, month and year.

I frequently hear persons in old age say how they would live, if they were to live their lives over again: Resolved, That I will live just so as I can think I shall wish I had done, supposing I live to old age.

Resolved, To endeavour, to my utmost, so to act, as I can think I should do, if I had already seen the happiness of heaven and hell's torments.

Resolved, Never to give over, nor in the least

to slacken, my fight with my corruptions, however unsuccessful I may be.

Resolved, Never to do anything, which I should be afraid to do, if I expected it would not be above an hour before I should hear the last trump.

Let there be something of benevolence in all that I speak.

appendix B

This is the complete text of Jonathan Edwards's noteworthy sermon "Sinners in the Hands of an Angry God," preached at Enfield, Connecticut on July 8, 1741.

Their foot shall slide in due time. (Deut. 32:35)

1. In this verse is threatened the vengeance of God on the wicked unbelieving Israelites, who were God's visible people, and who lived under the means of grace; but who, notwithstanding all God's wonderful works towards them, remained (as ver. 28.) void of counsel, having no understanding in them. Under all the cultivations of heaven, they brought forth bitter and poisonous fruit; as in the two verses next preceding the text. The expression I have chosen for my text, Their

foot shall slide in due time, seems to imply the following doings, relating to the punishment and destruction to which these wicked Israelites were exposed. That they were always exposed to *destruction;* as one that stands or walks in slippery places is always exposed to fall. This is implied in the manner of their destruction coming upon them, being represented by their foot sliding. The same is expressed, Psalm 73:18. "Surely thou didst set them in slippery places: thou castedst them down into destruction."

2. It implies, that they were always exposed to sudden unexpected destruction. As he that walks in slippery places is every moment liable to fall, he cannot foresee one moment whether he shall stand or fall the next; and when he does fall, he falls at once without warning: Which is also expressed in Psalm 73:18-19. "Surely thou didst set them in slippery places: thou castedst them down into destruction. How are they brought into desolation, as in a moment!"

3. Another thing implied is, that they are liable to fall *of themselves,* without being thrown down by the hand of another; as he that stands or walks on slippery ground needs nothing but his own weight to throw him down.

4. That the reason why they are not fallen already, and do not fall now, is only that God's appointed time

is not come. For it is said, that when that due time, or appointed time comes, *their foot shall slide.* Then they shall be left to fall, as they are inclined by their own weight. God will not hold them up in these slippery places any longer, but will let them go; and then at that very instant, they shall fall into destruction; as he that stands on such slippery declining ground, on the edge of a pit, he cannot stand alone, when he is let go he immediately falls and is lost. The observation from the words that I would now insist upon is this. "There is nothing that keeps wicked men at any one moment out of hell, but the mere pleasure of God." By the mere pleasure of God, I mean His sovereign pleasure, His arbitrary will, restrained by no obligation, hindered by no manner of difficulty, any more than if nothing else but God's mere will had in the least degree, or in any respect whatsoever, any hand in the preservation of wicked men one moment. The truth of this observation may appear by the following considerations.

1. There is no want of *power* in God to cast wicked men into hell at any moment. Men's hands cannot be strong when God rises up. The strongest have no power to resist Him, nor can any deliver out of His hands.—He is not only able to cast wicked men into hell, but He can most easily do it. Sometimes an earthly prince meets with a great deal of difficulty to subdue a rebel, who has found means to fortify himself, and has made himself

strong by the numbers of his followers. But it is not so with God. There is no fortress that is any defence from the power of God. Though hand join in hand, and vast multitudes of God's enemies combine and associate themselves, they are easily broken in pieces. They are as great heaps of light chaff before the whirlwind; or large quantities of dry stubble before devouring flames. We find it easy to tread on and crush a worm that we see crawling on the earth; so it is easy for us to cut or singe a slender thread that any thing hangs by: thus easy is it for God, when He pleases, to cast His enemies down to hell. What are we, that we should think to stand before Him, at whose rebuke the earth trembles, and before whom the rocks are thrown down?

2. They *deserve* to be cast into hell; so that divine justice never stands in the way, it makes no objection against God's using His power at any moment to destroy them. Yea, on the contrary, justice calls aloud for an infinite punishment of their sins. Divine justice says of the tree that brings forth such grapes of Sodom, "Cut it down; why cumbereth it the ground?" Luke 13:7. The sword of divine justice is every moment brandished over their heads, and it is nothing but the hand of arbitrary mercy, and God's mere will, that holds it back.

3. They are already under a sentence of *condemnation* to hell. They do not only justly deserve to be

cast down thither, but the sentence of the law of God, that eternal and immutable rule of righteousness that God has fixed between Him and mankind, is gone out against them, and stands against them; so that they are bound over already to hell. John 3:18. "He that believeth not is condemned already." So that every unconverted man properly belongs to hell; that is his place; from thence he is, John 8:23. "Ye are from beneath." And thither be is bound; it is the place that justice, and God's word, and the sentence of His unchangeable law assign to him.

4. They are now the objects of that very same anger and wrath of God, that is expressed in the torments of hell. And the reason why they do not go down to hell at each moment, is not because God, in whose power they are, is not then very angry with them; as He is with many miserable creatures now tormented in hell, who there feel and bear the fierceness of His wrath. Yea, God is a great deal more angry with great numbers that are now on earth: yea, doubtless, with many that are now in this congregation, who it may be are at ease, than He is with many of those who are now in the flames of hell. So that it is not because God is unmindful of their wickedness, and does not resent it, that He does not let loose His hand and cut them off. God is not altogether such an one as themselves, though they may imagine Him to be so. The wrath of God burns against them, their damnation does not

slumber; the pit is prepared, the fire is made ready, the furnace is now hot, ready to receive them; the flames do now rage and glow. The glittering sword is whet, and held over them, and the pit hath opened its mouth under them.

5. The *devil* stands ready to fall upon them, and seize them as his own, at what moment God shall permit him. They belong to him; he has their souls in his possession, and under his dominion. The scripture represents them as his goods, Luke 11:12. The devils watch them; they are ever by them at their right hand; they stand waiting for them, like greedy hungry lions that see their prey, and expect to have it, but are for the present kept back. If God should withdraw His hand, by which they are restrained, they would in one moment fly upon their poor souls. The old serpent is gaping for them; hell opens its mouth wide to receive them; and if God should permit it, they would be hastily swallowed up and lost.

6. There are in the souls of wicked men those hellish principles reigning, that would presently kindle and flame out into hell fire, if it were not for God's restraints. There is laid in the very nature of carnal men, a foundation for the torments of hell. There are those corrupt principles, in reigning power in them, and in full possession of them, that are seeds of hell fire. These principles are active and powerful, exceeding violent in their nature, and if it were

not for the restraining hand of God upon them,
they would soon break out, they would flame out
after the same manner as the same corruptions, the
same enmity does in the hearts of damned souls,
and would beget the same torments as they do in
them. The souls of the wicked are in scripture
compared to the troubled sea, Isa. 57:20. For the
present, God restrains their wickedness by His
mighty power, as He does the raging waves of the
troubled sea, saying, "Hitherto shalt thou come,
but no further;" but if God should withdraw that
restraining power, it would soon carry all before it.
Sin is the ruin and misery of the soul; it is destruc-
tive in its nature; and if God should leave it without restraint, there would need nothing else to
make the soul perfectly miserable. The corruption
of the heart of man is immoderate and boundless
in its fury; and while wicked men live here, it is
like fire pent up by God's restraints, whereas if it
were let loose, it would set on fire the course of
nature; and as the heart is now a sink of sin, so if
sin was not restrained, it would immediately turn
the soul into a fiery oven, or a furnace of fire and
brimstone.

7. It is no security to wicked men for one moment,
that there are no visible means of death at hand. It
is no security to a natural man, that he is now in
health, and that he does not see which way he
should now immediately go out of the world by
any accident, and that there is no visible danger in

any respect in his circumstances. The manifold and continual experience of the world in all ages, shows this is no evidence, that a man is not on the very brink of eternity, and that the next step will not be into another world. The unseen, unthought-of ways and means of persons going suddenly out of the world are innumerable and inconceivable. Unconverted men walk over the pit of hell on a rotten covering, and there are innumerable places in this covering so weak that they will not bear their weight, and these places are not seen. The arrows of death fly unseen at noon-day; the sharpest sight cannot discern them. God has so many different unsearchable ways of taking wicked men out of the world and sending them to hell, that there is nothing to make it appear, that God had need to be at the expence of a miracle, or go out of the ordinary course of His providence, to destroy any wicked man, at any moment. All the means that there are of sinners going out of the world, are so in God's hands, and so universally and absolutely subject to His power and determination, that it does not depend at all the less on the mere will of God, whether sinners shall at any moment go to hell, than if means were never made use of, or at all concerned in the case.

8. Natural men's prudence and care to preserve their own lives, or the care of others to preserve them, do not secure them a moment. To this, divine providence and universal experience do also bear

testimony. There is this clear evidence that men's own wisdom is no security to them from death; that if it were otherwise we should see some difference between the wise and politic men of the world, and others, with regard to their liableness to early and unexpected death: but how is it in fact? Eccles. 2:16. "How dieth the wise man? as the fool."

9. All wicked men's pains and *contrivance* which they use to escape hell, while they continue to reject Christ, and so remain wicked men, do not secure them from hell one moment. Almost every natural man that hears of hell, flatters himself that he shall escape it; he depends upon himself for his own security; he flatters himself in what he has done, in what he is now doing, or what he intends to do. Every one lays out matters in his own mind how he shall avoid damnation, and flatters himself that he contrives well for himself, and that his schemes will not fail. They hear indeed that there are but few saved, and that the greater part of men that have died heretofore are gone to hell; but each one imagines that he lays out matters better for his own escape than others have done. He does not intend to come to that place of torment; he says within himself, that he intends to take effectual care, and to order matters so for himself as not to fail. But the foolish children of men miserably delude themselves in their own schemes, and in confidence in their own strength and wisdom;

they trust to nothing but a shadow. The greater part of those who heretofore have lived under the same means of grace, and are now dead, are undoubtedly gone to hell; and it was not because they were not as wise as those who are now alive: it was not because they did not lay out matters as well for themselves to secure their own escape. If we could speak with them, and inquire of them, one by one, whether they expected, when alive, and when they used to hear about hell ever to be the subects of that misery: we doubtless, should hear one and another reply, "No, I never intended to come here: I had laid out matters otherwise in my mind; I thought I should contrive well for myself: I thought my scheme good. I intended to take effectual care; but it came upon me unexpected; I did not look for it at that time, and in that manner; it came as a thief: Death outwitted me: God's wrath was too quick for me. Oh, my cursed foolishness! I was flattering myself, and pleasing myself with vain dreams of what I would do hereafter; and when I was saying, Peace and safety, then suddenly destruction came upon me.

10. God has laid Himself under *no obligation,* by any promise to keep any natural man out of hell one moment. God certainly has made no promises either of eternal life, or of any deliverance or preservation from eternal death, but what are contained in the covenant of grace, the promises that are given in Christ, in whom all the promises are

yea and amen. But surely they have no interest in the promises of the covenant of grace who are not the children of the covenant, who do not believe in any of the promises, and have no interest in the Mediator of the covenant. So that, whatever some have imagined and pretended about promises made to natural men's earnest seeking and knocking, it is plain and manifest, that whatever pains a natural man takes in religion, whatever prayers he makes, till he believes in Christ, God is under no manner of obligation to keep him a moment from eternal destruction. So that, thus it is that natural men are held in the hand of God, over the pit of hell; they have deserved the fiery pit, and are already sentenced to it; and God is dreadfully provoked, His anger is as great towards them as to those that are actually suffering the executions of the fierceness of His wrath in hell, and they have done nothing in the least to appease or abate that anger, neither is God in the least bound by any promise to hold them up one moment; the devil is waiting for them, hell is gaping for them, the flames gather and flash about them, and would fain lay hold on them, and swallow them up; the fire pent up in their own hearts is struggling to break out: and they have no interest in any Mediator, there are no means within reach that can be any security to them. In short, they have no refuge, nothing to take hold of, all that preserves them every moment is the mere arbitrary will, and uncovenanted, unobliged forbearance of an incensed God.

Application

The use of this awful subject may be for awakening unconverted persons in this congregation. This that you have heard is the case of every one of you that are out of Christ.—That world of misery, that lake of burning brimstone, is extended abroad under you. There is the dreadful pit of the glowing flames of the wrath of God; there is hell's wide gaping mouth open; and you have nothing to stand upon, nor any thing to take hold of, there is nothing between you and hell but the air; it is only the power and mere pleasure of God that holds you up. You probably are not sensible of this; you find you are kept out of hell, but do not see the hand of God in it; but look at other things, as the good state of your bodily constitution, your care of your own life, and the means you use for your own preservation. But indeed these things are nothing; if God should withdraw his band, they would avail no more to keep you from falling, than the thin air to hold up a person that is suspended in it. Your wickedness makes you as it were heavy as lead, and to tend downwards with great weight and pressure towards hell; and if God should let you go, you would immediately sink and swiftly descend and plunge into the bottomless gulf, and your healthy constitution, and your own care and prudence, and best contrivance, and all your righteousness, would have no more influence to uphold you and keep you out of hell, than a spider's web would have to stop a falling rock. Were it not for the sovereign pleasure of God, the earth would not bear you one moment; for you are a burden to it; the creation groans with you; the creature is made subject to the bondage of your corruption, not willingly; the sun does not willingly shine upon you to give you light to serve sin and Satan; the earth does not willingly yield her increase to satisfy your lusts; nor is it willingly a stage for your wickedness to be acted upon; the air does not willingly serve you for breath to maintain the flame of life in your vitals, while you spend your life in the service of God's enemies. God's creatures are good, and were made for men to serve God with, and do not willingly subserve to any other purpose, and groan when they are abused to purposes so directly contrary to their nature and end. And the world would spew you out, were it not for the sovereign hand of Him who hath subjected it in hope. There are black clouds of God's wrath now hanging directly over your heads, full of the dreadful storm, and big with thunder; and were it not for the restraining hand of God, it would immediately burst forth upon you. The sovereign pleasure of God, for the present, stays His rough wind; otherwise it would come with fury, and your destruction would come like a whirlwind, and you would be like the chaff of the summer threshing floor. The wrath of God is like great waters that are dammed for the present; they increase more and more, and rise higher and higher, till an outlet is given; and the longer the stream is stopped, the more rapid and mighty is its course, when once it is let loose. It is true, that judgment against your evil works has not been executed hitherto; the floods of God's vengeance have been withheld; but your guilt in the mean time is constantly increasing, and you are every day treasuring up more wrath; the waters are constantly rising, and waxing more and more mighty; and there is nothing but the mere pleasure of God, that holds the waters back, that are un-willing to be stopped, and press hard to go forward. If God should only withdraw His hand from the flood-gate, it would immediately fly open, and the fiery floods of the fierceness and wrath of God, would rush forth with inconceivable fury, and would come upon you with omnipotent power; and if your strength were ten thousand times greater than it is, yea, ten thousand times greater than the strength of the stoutest, sturdiest devil in hell, it would be nothing to withstand or endure it. The bow of God's wrath is bent, and the arrow made ready on the string, and justice bends the arrow at your heart, and strains the bow, and it is nothing but the mere pleasure of God, and that of an angry God, without any promise or obligation at all, that keeps the arrow one moment from being made drunk with your blood. Thus all you that never passed under a great change of heart, by the mighty power of the Spirit of God upon your souls; all you that were never born again, and made new creatures, and raised from being dead in sin, to a state of new, and before altogether unexperienced light and life, are in the hands of an angry God. However you may have reformed your life in many things, and may have had religious affections, and may keep up a form of religion in your families and closets, and in the house of God, it is nothing but His mere pleasure that keeps you from being this moment swallowed up in everlasting destruction. However unconvinced you may now be of the truth of what you hear, by and by you will be fully convinced of it. Those that are gone from being in the like circumstances with you, see that it was so with them; for destruction came suddenly upon most of them; when they expected nothing of it, and while they were saying, Peace and safety: now they see, that those things on which they depended for peace and safety, were nothing but thin air and empty shadows. The God that holds you over the pit of hell, much as one holds a spider, or some loathsome insect over the fire, abhors you, and is dreadfully provoked: His wrath towards you burns like fire; He looks upon you as worthy of nothing else, but to be cast into the fire; He is of purer eyes than to bear to have you in His sight; you are ten thousand times more abominable in His eyes, than the most hateful venomous serpent is in ours. You have offended Him infinitely more than ever a stubborn rebel did his prince; and yet it is nothing but His hand that holds you from falling into the fire every moment. It is to be ascribed to nothing else, that you did not go to hell the last night; that you was suffered to awake again in this world, after you closed your eyes to sleep. And there is no other reason to be given, why you have not dropped into hell since you arose in the morning, but that God's hand has held you up. There is no other reason to be given why you have not gone to hell, since you have sat here in the house of God, provoking His pure eyes by your sinful wicked manner of attending His solemn worship. Yea, there is nothing else that is to be given as a reason why you do not this very moment drop down into hell. O sinner! Consider the fearful danger you are in: it is a great furnace of wrath, a wide and bottomless pit, full of the fire of wrath, that you are held over in the hand of that God, whose wrath is provoked and incensed as much against you, as against many of the damned in hell. You hang by a slender thread, with the flames of divine wrath flashing about it, and ready every moment to singe it, and burn it asunder; and you have no interest in any Mediator, and nothing to lay hold of to save yourself, nothing to keep off the flames of wrath, nothing of your own, nothing that you ever have done, nothing that you can do, to induce God to spare you one moment. And consider here more particularly

1. *Whose* wrath it is: it is the wrath of the infinite God. If it were only the wrath of man, though it were of the most potent prince, it would be comparatively little to be regarded. The wrath of kings is very much dreaded, especially of absolute monarchs, who have the possessions and lives of their subjects wholly in their power, to be disposed of at their mere will. Prov. 20:2. "The fear of a king is as the roaring of a lion: whoso provoketh him to anger, sinneth against his own soul." The subject that very much enrages an arbitrary prince, is liable to suffer the most extreme torments that human art can invent, or human power can inflict. But the greatest earthly potentates in their greatest majesty and strength, and when clothed in their greatest terrors, are but feeble, despicable worms of the dust, in comparison of the great and almighty Creator and King of heaven and earth. It is but little that they can do, when most enraged, and when they have exerted the utmost of their fury. All the kings of the earth, before God, are as grasshoppers; they are nothing, and less than nothing: both their love

and their hatred is to be despised. The wrath of the great King of kings, is as much more terrible than theirs, as His majesty is greater. Luke 12:4–5. "And I say unto you my friends, Be not afraid of them that kill the body, and after that have no more that they can do. But I will forewarn you whom ye shall fear: Fear him, which after he hath killed hath power to cast into hell; yea, I say unto you, Fear him."

2. It is the *fierceness* of His wrath that you are exposed to. We often read of the fury of God; as in Isaiah 59:18. "According to their deeds, accordingly he will repay, fury to his adversaries." So Isaiah 66:15. "For behold, the Lord will come with fire, and with his chariots like a whirlwind, to render his anger with fury, and his rebuke with flames of fire." And in many other places. So, Rev. 19:15, we read of "the winepress of the fierceness and wrath of Almighty God." The words are exceeding terrible. If it had only been said, "the wrath of God," the words would have implied that which is infinitely dreadful: but it is "the fierceness and wrath of God." The fury of God! The fierceness of Jehovah! Oh, how dreadful must that be! Who can utter or conceive what such expressions carry in them! But it is also "the fierceness and wrath of *Almighty* God." As though there would be a very great manifestation of His almighty power in what the fierceness of His wrath should inflict, as though omnipotence should be as

it were enraged, and exerted, as men are wont to exert their strength in the fierceness of their wrath. Oh! then, what will be the consequence! What will become of the poor worms that shall suffer it! Whose hands can be strong? And whose heart can endure? To what a dreadful, inexpressible, inconceivable depth of misery must the poor creature be sunk who shall be the subject of this! Consider this, you that are here present, that yet remain in an unregenerate state. That God will execute the fierceness of His anger, implies, that He will inflict wrath without any pity. When God beholds the ineffable extremity of your case, and sees your torment to be so vastly disproportioned to your strength, and sees how your poor soul is crushed, and sinks down, as it were, into an infinite gloom; He will have no compassion upon you, He will not forbear the executions of His wrath, or in the least lighten His hand; there shall be no moderation or mercy, nor will God then at all stay His rough wind; He will have no regard to your welfare, nor be at all careful lest you should suffer too much in any other sense, than only that you shall *not suffer beyond what strict justice requires*. Nothing shall be withheld, because it is so hard for you to bear. Ezek. 8:18. "Therefore will I also deal in fury: mine eye shall not spare, neither will I have pity: and though they cry in mine ears with a loud voice, yet will I not hear them." Now God stands ready to pity you; this is a day of mercy; you may cry now with some encouragement of obtaining mercy. But when once the day of mercy is past, your most lamentable and dolorous cries and shrieks will be in vain; you will be wholly lost and thrown away of God, as to any regard to your welfare. God will have no other use to put you to, but to suffer misery; you shall be continued in being to no other end; for you will be a vessel of wrath fitted to destruction; and there will be no other use of this vessel, but to be filled full of wrath. God will be so far from pitying you when you cry to Him, that it is said He will only "laugh and mock," Prov. 1:25–26, &c. How awful are those words, Isa. 63:3, which are the words of the great God. "I will tread them in mine anger, and trample them in my fury; and their blood shall be sprinkled upon my garments, and I will stain all my raiment." It is perhaps impossible to conceive of words that carry in them greater manifestations of these three things, *vis.* contempt, and hatred, and fierceness of indignation. If you cry to God to pity you, He will be so far from pitying you in your doleful case, or showing you the least regard or favour, that instead of that, He will only tread you under foot. And though He will know that you cannot bear the weight of omnipotence treading upon you, yet He will not regard that, but He will crush you under His feet without mercy; He will crush out your blood, and make it fly, and it shall be sprinkled on His garments, so as to stain all His raiment. He will not only hate you, but He will have you, in the utmost contempt: no place shall be thought fit for you, but under His feet to be trodden down as the mire of the streets. The misery you are exposed to is that which God will inflict to that end, that He might show what that wrath of Jehovah is. God hath had it on His heart to show to angels and men, both how excellent His love is, and also how terrible His wrath is. Sometimes earthly kings have a mind to show how terrible their wrath is, by the extreme punishments they would execute on those that would provoke them. Nebuchadnezzar, that mighty and haughty monarch of the Chaldean empire, was willing to show his wrath when enraged with Shadrach, Meshech, and Abednego; and accordingly gave orders that the burning fiery furnace should be heated seven times hotter than it was before; doubtless, it was raised to the utmost degree of fierceness that human art could raise it. But the great God is also willing to show His wrath, and magnify His awful majesty and mighty power in the extreme sufferings of His enemies. Rom. 9:22. "What if God, willing to shew his wrath, and to make his power known, endured with much longsuffering the vessels of wrath fitted to destruction." And seeing this is His design, and what He has determined, even to show how terrible the unrestrained wrath, the fury and fierceness of Jehovah is, He will do it to effect. There will be something accomplished and brought to pass that will be dreadful with a witness. When the great and angry God hath risen up and executed His awful vengeance on the poor sinner, and the wretch is actually suffering the infinite weight and power of His indignation, then will God call upon the whole universe to behold that awful majesty and mighty power that is to be seen in it. Isa. 33:12–14. "And the people shall be as the burnings of lime: as thorns cut up shall they be burnt in the fire. Hear, ye that are far off, what I have done; and, ye that are near, acknowledge my might. The sinners in Zion are afraid; fearfulness hath surprised the hypocrites," &c. Thus it will be with you that are in an unconverted state, if you continue in it; the infinite might, and majesty, and terribleness of the omnipotent God shall be magnified upon you, in the ineffable strength of your torments. You shall be tormented in the presence of the holy angels, and in the presence of the Lamb; and when you shall be in this state of suffering, the glorious inhabitants of heaven shall go forth and look on the awful spectacle, that they may see what the wrath and fierceness of the Almighty is; and when they have seen it, they will fall down and adore that great power and majesty. Isa. 66:23–24. "And it shall come to pass, that from one new moon to another, and from one sabbath to another, shall all flesh come to worship before me, saith the Lord. And they shall go forth, and look upon the carcases of the men that have transgressed against me: for their worm shall not die, neither shall their fire be quenched; and they shall be an abhorring unto all flesh."

4. It is *everlasting* wrath. It would be dreadful to suffer

this fierceness and wrath of Almighty God one moment; but you must suffer it to all eternity. There will be no end to this exquisite horrible misery. When you look forward, you shall see a long for ever, a boundless duration before you, which will swallow up your thoughts, and amaze your soul; and you will absolutely despair of ever having any deliverance, any end, any mitigation, any rest at all. You will know certainly that you must wear out long ages, millions of millions of ages, in wrestling and conflicting with this almighty merciless vengeance; and then when you have so done, when so many ages have actually been spent by you in this manner, you will know that all is but a point to what remains. So that your punishment will indeed be infinite. Oh, who can express what the state of a soul in such circumstances is! All that we can possibly say about it, gives but a very feeble, faint representation of it; it is inexpressible and inconceivable: For "who knows the power of God's anger?" How dreadful is the state of those that are daily and hourly in the danger of this great wrath and infinite misery! But this is the dismal case of every soul in this congregation that has not been born again, however moral and strict, sober and religious, they may otherwise be. Oh that you would consider it, whether you be young or old! There is reason to think, that there are many in this congregation now hearing this discourse, that will actually be the subjects of this very misery to all eternity. We know not who they are, or in what seats they sit, or what thoughts they now have. It may be they are now at ease, and hear all these things without much disturbance, and are now flattering themselves that they are not the persons, promising themselves that they shall escape. If we knew that there was one person, and but one, in the whole congregation, that was to be the subject of this misery, what an awful thing would it be to think of! If we knew who it was, what an awful sight would it be to see such a person! How might all the rest of the congregation lift up a lamentable and bitter cry over him! But, alas! instead of one, how many is it likely will remember this discourse in hell? And it would be a wonder, if some that are now present should not be in hell in a very short time, even before this year is out. And it would be no wonder if some persons, that now sit here, in some seats of this meetinghouse, in health, quiet and secure, should be there before tomorrow morning. Those of you that finally continue in a natural condition, that shall keep out of hell longest will be there in a little time! Your damnation does not slumber; it will come swiftly, and, in all probability, very suddenly upon many of you. You have reason to wonder that you are not already in hell. It is doubtless the case of some whom you have seen and known, that never deserved hell more than you, and that heretofore appeared as likely to have been now alive as you. Their case is past all hope; they are crying in extreme misery and perfect despair; but here you are in the land of the living and in the house of God, and have an opportunity to obtain salvation. What would not those poor damned hopeless souls give for one day's opportunity such as you now enjoy! And now you have an extraordinary opportunity, a day wherein Christ has thrown the door of mercy wide open, and stands in calling and crying with a loud voice to poor sinners; a day wherein many are flocking to Him, and pressing into the kingdom of God. Many are daily coming from the east, west, north and south; many that were very lately in the same miserable condition that you are in, are now in a happy state, with their hearts filled with love to Him who has loved them, and washed them from their sins in His own blood, and rejoicing in hope of the glory of God. How awful is it to be left behind at such a day! To see so many others feasting, while you are pining and perishing! To see so many rejoicing and singing for joy of heart, while you have cause to mourn for sorrow of heart, and howl for vexation of spirit! How can you rest one moment in such a condition? Are not your souls as precious as the souls of the people at Suffield, where they are flocking from day to day to Christ? Are there not many here who have lived long in the world, and are not to this day born again? And so are aliens from the commonwealth of Israel, and have done nothing ever since they have lived, but treasure up wrath against the day of wrath? Oh, sirs, your case, in an especial manner, is extremely dangerous. Your guilt and hardness of heart is extremely great.

Do you not see how generally persons of your years are passed over and left, in the present remarkable and wonderful dispensation of God's mercy? You had need to consider yourselves, and awake thoroughly out of sleep. You cannot bear the fierceness and wrath of the infinite God.—And you, young men, and young women, will you neglect this precious season which you now enjoy, when so many others of your age are renouncing all youthful vanities, and flocking to Christ? You especially have now an extraordinary opportunity; but if you neglect it, it will soon be with you as with those persons who spent all the precious days of youth in sin, and are now come to such a dreadful pass in blindness and hardness. And you, children, who are unconverted, do not you know that you are going down to hell, to bear the dreadful wrath of that God, who is now angry with you every day and every night? Will you be content to be the children of the devil, when so many other children in the land are converted, and are become the holy and happy children of the King of kings? And let every one that is yet out of Christ, and hanging over the pit of hell, whether they be old men and women, or middle aged, or young people, or little children, now hearken to the loud calls of God's word and providence. This acceptable year of the Lord, a day of such great favours to some, will doubtless be a day of as remarkable vengeance to others. Men's hearts harden, and their guilt increases apace at such a day as this, if they neglect their souls; and never was there so great danger of such persons being given up to hardness of heart and blindness of mind. God seems now to be hastily gathering in His elect in all parts of the land; and probably the greater part of adult persons that ever shall be saved, will be brought in now in a little time, and that it will be as it was on the great out-pouring of the Spirit upon the Jews in the apostles' days; the election will obtain, and the rest will be blinded. If this should be the case with you, you will eternally curse this day, and will curse the day that ever you was born, to see such a season of the pouring out of God's Spirit, and will wish that you had died and gone to hell before you had seen it. Now undoubtedly it is, as it was in the days of John the Baptist, the axe is in an extraordinary manner laid at the root of the trees, that every tree which brings not forth good fruit, may be hewn down and cast into the fire. Therefore, let every one that is out of Christ, now awake and fly from the wrath to come. The wrath of Almighty God is now undoubtedly hanging over a great part of this congregation: Let every one fly out of Sodom: "Haste and escape for your lives, look not behind you, escape to the mountain, lest you be consumed."

Bibliography

Davidson, Edward H., *Jonathan Edwards, the Narrative of a Puritan Mind.* Boston: Houghton Mifflin Co. 1966.

Edwards, Jonathan, ed., *The Life of Rev. David Brainerd.* Grand Rapids, MI: Baker Book House, 1978.

Ferm, Vergilius, *Puritan Sage: Collected Writings of Jonathan Edwards.* New York: Library Publishers, 1953.

Griffin, Edward M., *Jonathan Edwards.* Minneapolis: University of Minnesota Press, Pamphlet No. 97, Minnesota University Pamphlets on American Writers, 1971.

Levin, David, ed., *Jonathan Edwards A Profile.* New York: Hill and Wang, 1969.

McGrath, Alister E., *A Cloud of Witnesses.* Grand Rapids, MI: Zondervan Publishing House, 1990.

Miller, Perry, *Jonathan Edwards.* New York: Meridian Books, The World Publishing Company, 1959.

Murray, Iain H., *Jonathan Edwards, A New Biography.* Carlisle, PA: The Banner of Truth Trust, 1987.

Parkes, Henry Bamford, *Jonathan Edwards, The Fiery Puritan.* New York: Minton, Balch & Company, 1930.

Simonson, Harold P., *Jonathan Edwards: Theologian of the Heart.* Grand Rapids, MI: Wm. B. Eerdmans Publishing Co., 1974.

Smith, John E., *Jonathan Edwards: Puritan, Preacher, Philosopher.* London: Geoffrey Chapman, An imprint of Cassell Publishers Limited Villiers House, 1992.

Stein, Stephen J., *Jonathan Edwards's Writings.* Bloomington and Indianapolis, IN: Indiana University Press, 1996.

Tracy, Patricia J., *Jonathan Edwards, Pastor: Religion and Society in Eighteenth-Century Northampton.* New York: American Century Series, Hill and Wang, A Division of Farrar, Straus and Giroux, 1979–1980.

Turnbull, Ralph G., *Jonathan Edwards The Preacher.* Grand Rapids, MI: Baker Book House, 1958.

Winslow, Ola Elizabeth, *Jonathan Edwards, 1703–1758, A Biography.* New York: The Macmillan Co., 1940.